October 11–13, 2012
Calgary, Alberta, Canada

I0030643

**Association for
Computing Machinery**

Advancing Computing as a Science & Profession

RIIT'12

Proceedings of the ACM

Research in Information Technology

Sponsored by:
ACM SIGITE

Supported by:
Academic Alliance, Piazza, and Mount Royal University

Association for Computing Machinery

Advancing Computing as a Science & Profession

The Association for Computing Machinery
2 Penn Plaza, Suite 701
New York, New York 10121-0701

ISBN: 978-1-4503-1643-9 (Digital)

ISBN: 978-1-4503-1924-9 (Print)

Additional copies may be ordered prepaid from:

ACM Order Department
PO Box 30777
New York, NY 10087-0777, USA

Phone: 1-800-342-6626 (USA and Canada)
+1-212-626-0500 (Global)
Fax: +1-212-944-1318
E-mail: acmhelp@acm.org
Hours of Operation: 8:30 am – 4:30 pm ET

Printed in the USA

SIGITE/RIIT 2012 Chair's Welcome

Welcome to Calgary and Mount Royal University!

It is our great pleasure to host the 13th Annual Conference on Information Technology Education and the 1st Annual Research in IT Conference. This year is especially exciting since it introduces the brand new IT Research conference; our aim in this and in future joint SIGITE/RIIT conferences is to provide a venue for showcasing research in information technology along with our traditional focus on teaching IT. Inspired by the new research conference, our joint conference has the theme of *Working Together: Research & Education for IT*.

Over the years, we have found the SIGITE conference to be both a wellspring of ideas to address issues such as the above and a much-needed opportunity to network and bond with fellow IT educators. We hope you find this year's conference as beneficial and rewarding as the many we have attended in the past.

We are truly fortunate this year to have Randy Thompson of Venture Alberta as our keynote speaker. Randy provides a keynote that combines our interest in both IT education and IT research. Integrating his many years of experience at the head of an IT angel investors group, Randy shows us how IT departments in universities can play a key role in commercializing IT research and thereby improve local economies as well as IT education.

SIGITE/RIIT 2012 is truly a team effort, and we would like to acknowledge and thank Dave Armitage as Program Chair for SIGITE. Dave was last year's Sponsorship Chair so he has been deeply involved with the conference organization for over a year. We are also very indebted to Jeffrey Brewer, who had the very difficult task of being the inaugural Program Chair for RIIT, which necessitated not only navigating many uncharted waters at ACM but also organizing reviewers and the conference schedule for both SIGITE and RIIT. We would also like to thank Rob Friedman for his successful efforts as Sponsorship Chair, Mark Stockman for his leadership and guidance as SIGITE Chair, and all of our sponsors for their generous support of this event.

We would also like to thank the many people who worked so hard behind the scenes on the many administrative challenges and needs. These include Bill Paterson as Local Arrangements Chair, Faith-Michael Uzoka as Finance and Registration Chair, April Mosqus at ACM for assistance with overall planning, Lisa Tolles at Sheridan Printing Company for organizing the proceedings, Jeane Vincent at the University of South Florida for the graphic design work on the conference program, and Henry Walker for administering the paper reviewing submission system.

We hope that you will find the conference's program to be both inspiring and thought-provoking and that the conference will provide you with a valuable opportunity to share ideas with other researchers and practitioners from institutions around the world.

Randy Connolly
SIGITE/RIIT '12 Conference Chair
Mount Royal University, Canada

SIGITE/RIIT 2012 Program Chairs' Message

Being part of something new is always a great experience, and this year's inauguration of the Research in Information Technology (RIIT) conference as a new companion to the more "venerable" SIGITE conference is no exception. The dual conference theme, *Working Together: Research & Education for IT*, emphasizes the increasing synergy between teaching and research in our field. It's a long-standing principle among academics that research should inform our teaching; over years of SIGITE conferences, we've demonstrated the bi-directionality of that relationship, as teaching has often generated the source data and motivation for our research in IT education.

A strong motivation for launching RIIT was the need to recognize "research in IT" as more than a fragmented collection of pursuits in other computing disciplines. We have been watching a body of research develop that is uniquely characteristic of information technology. With a hands-on flavor and stronger connections with industry, it is clearly differentiating itself from research in more traditional computing disciplines, and is deserving of its own conference venue.

We have a selection of exceptionally strong papers this year. Making final choices of papers for presentation was anything but easy, and many quality papers could not be included due to the constraints inherent in a conference schedule. We received a total of 87 paper submissions, 18 of which were classified as RIIT submissions and the rest (69) as SIGITE submissions. Papers received a minimum of three reviews, with approximately 4.6 reviews per paper being the mean. We had a shorter than usual review time available for this year's conferences; a large and enthusiastic group of reviewers – 134 of you! – were instrumental in getting the job done. Each reviewer handled from one to eight papers; the mean was approximately three papers per reviewer. A total of 402 reviews were submitted. Additional recognition and thanks must go to a self-sacrificing subset of reviewers who took on emergency reviews with turnaround times of less than two days.

Of the eighteen paper sessions at the dual conference, four of them feature RIIT papers, while fourteen present SIGITE papers. Nine of the forty-nine papers to be presented represent RIIT submissions; one accepted RIIT paper was withdrawn after notification. While twenty percent of accepted papers coming from RIIT submissions is a respectable number for the first year of the conference, we look forward to building on that in 2013 and beyond. We need to spread the word to our non-IT education colleagues that RIIT is open for business and will be a welcoming venue.

We have some great panel sessions on the conference schedule. At thirty minutes each, you will find concentrated discussions of significant issues by highly qualified panelists. And don't miss Thursday afternoon's opportunity to view the six posters selected for our conferences.

Welcome to RIIT 2012 and SIGITE 2012. Hear about the latest research in our field, meet new colleagues and link up again with old friends. And, of course, start looking forward to SIGITE/RIIT 2013. Thanks for attending!

Dave Armitage
SIGITE'12 Program Chair
University of South Florida

Jeff Brewer
RIIT'12 Program Chair
Purdue University

Table of Contents

SIGITE/RIIT 2012 Conference Organization vi

SIGITE/RIIT 2012 Reviewers vii

SIGITE/RIIT 2012 Sponsor and Supporters ix

Session 1: IT Research (1)
Session Chair: Peter Alston *(Edge Hill University)*

- **Evaluations of AODV and DSR for QoS Requirements** 1
  Hetal Jasani *(Northern Kentucky University)*

- **Mapping the Cyber Security Terrain in a Research Context** 7
  Dale C. Rowe, Barry Lunt *(Brigham Young University)*

Session 2: IT Research (2)
Session Chair: Mark Stockman *(University of Cincinnati)*

- **Discovering Workplace Motivators for the Millennial Generation of IT Employees** 13
  Thomas E. Bunton, Jeffrey L. Brewer *(Purdue University)*

- **Identifying and Evaluating Information Technology Bachelor's Degree Programs** 19
  Barry M. Lunt, Bikalpa Neupane, Andrew Hansen, Richard Ofori *(Brigham Young University)*

- **Resource Utilization Prediction: A Proposal for Information Technology Research** 25
  Daniel W. Yoas *(Nova Southeastern University & Pennsylvania College of Technology)*,
  Greg Simco *(Nova Southeastern University)*

Session 3: IT Research (3)
Session Chair: Dave Armitage *(University of South Florida)*

- **Testing & Quantifying ERP Usability** 31
  Nancy E. Parks *(Bentley University)*

- **A Simulation-based Fuzzy Multi-Attribute Decision Making for Prioritizing
  Software Requirements** 37
  Abdel Ejnioui, Carlos E. Otero *(University of South Florida)*, Luis D. Otero *(Florida Institute of Technology)*

- **Comparison of VM Deployment Methods for HPC Education** 43
  Nicholas Robison, Thomas Hacker *(Purdue University)*

Panel Session

- **Defining IT Research** 49
  Rob Friedman *(University of Washington Tacoma)*, Han Reichgelt *(Southern Polytechnic State University)*,
  William W. Agresti *(The Johns Hopkins University)*, Mark Stockman *(University of Cincinnati)*,
  Joseph J. Ekstrom *(Brigham Young University)*

Session 4: IT Research (4)
Session Chair: Sam Chung *(University of Washington, Tacoma)*

- **A Survey of SCADA and Critical Infrastructure Incidents** 51
  Bill Miller, Dale C. Rowe *(Brigham Young University)*

- **Improving Accuracy in Face Tracking User Interfaces using Consumer Devices** 57
  Norman H. Villaroman, Dale C. Rowe *(Brigham Young University)*

Author Index 63

SIGITE/RIIT 2012 Conference Organization

General Chair: Randy Connolly, *Mount Royal University, Canada*

SIGITE Program Chair: William D. Armitage, *University of South Florida, USA*

RIIT Program Chair: Jeffrey L. Brewer, *Purdue University, USA*

Sponsorship Chair: Rob Friedman, *University of Washington, Tacoma, USA*

Local Arrangements Chair: Bill Paterson, *Mount Royal University, Canada*

Local Arrangements Committee: Alan Fedoruk, *Mount Royal University, Canada*
Charles Hepler, *Mount Royal University, Canada*
Namrata Khemka, *Mount Royal University, Canada*
Ricardo Hoar, *Mount Royal University, Canada*

Treasurer & Registration Chair: Faith-Michael Uzoka, *Mount Royal University, Canada*

Steering Committee Chair: Mark Stockman, *University of Cincinnati, USA*

Steering Committee: Jim Leone, *Rochester Institute of Technology, USA*
Terry Steinbach, *DePaul University, USA*
Barry Lunt, *Brigham Young University, USA*
Han Reichgelt, *Georgia Southern State University, USA*
Richard Helps, *Brigham Young University, USA*
Diane Delisio, *Miami University of Ohio, USA*
Mihaela Sabin, *University of New Hampshire, USA*
Daniel Benjamin, *American Public University System, USA*
Ken Baker, *University of Cincinnati, USA*
Rick L. Homkes, *Purdue University, USA*

SIGITE/RIIT 2012 Reviewers

Adnan Ahmad, *Massey University*

Sohaib Ahmed, *Massey University*

Syed Ishtiaque Ahmed, *Cornell University*

Mahir Ali, *University of Sharjah*

Hend Al-Khalifa, *King Saud University*

Fatima Al-Raisi, *Sultan Qaboos University*

Peter Alston, *Edge Hill University*

Jose Antonio Alvarez-Bermejo, *Universidad de Almeria*

William D. Armitage, *University of South Florida*

Alethe Bailey, *Newman University College*

Ken Baker, *University of Cincinnati*

William Barge, *Trine University*

Dianne Bills, *Rochester Institute of Technology*

Michael Black, *University of South Alabama*

Larry Booth, *Clayton State University*

Lynn Braender, *The College of New Jersey*

Wayne Brookes, *University of Technology, Sydney*

William Burkett, *Capella University School of Undergraduate Studies*

Rob Byrd, *Abilene Christian University*

Yu Cai, *Michigan Technological University*

Mario Camilleri, *University of Malta*

Peng-Wen Chen, *Oriental Institute of Technology*

Sam Chung, *University of Washington Tacoma*

Jean Coppola, *Pace University*

Monica Costa, *Instituto Politecnico de Castelo Branco*

Amanda Debler, *DIS AG*

Sonal Dekhane, *Georgia Gwinnett College*

Michele Dijkstra, *Pacific Lutheran University*

Nalaka Edirisinghe, *Temasek Polytechnic*

David Eggert, *University of New Haven*

Abdel Ejnioui, *University of South Florida*

Joseph Ekstrom, *Brigham Young University*

Stefano Federici, *Università di Cagliari*

Alan Fedoruk, *Mount Royal University*

Allan Fowler, *Waiariki Institute of Technology*

Robert Friedman, *University of Washington Tacoma*

Chunming Gao, *Michigan Technological University*

Daniel Garrison, *George Mason University*

Alessio Gaspar, *University of South Florida*

Angela Lemons, *North Carolina A&T State University*

Jim Leone, *Rochester Institute of Technology*

Chengcheng Li, *East Carolina University*

Sergio F. Lopes, *University of Minho*

David Luna, *Escola Superior de Tecnologia De Castelo Branco*

Phil Lunsford, *East Carolina University*

Barry Lunt, *Brigham Young University*

Cynthia Marcello, *SUNY Sullivan*

Kevin McReynolds, *LDS Business College*

Gabriele Meiselwitz, *Towson University*

Jose Metrolho, *Politecnic Institute of Castelo Branco*

Susan Miertschin, *University of Houston*

Trudi Miller, *University of Wisconsin - Stevens Point*

Craig Miller, *DePaul University*

Besim Mustafa, *Edge Hill University*

Rao Nemani, *The College of St. Scholastica*

Yin Pan, *Rochester Institute of Technology*

Bill Paterson, *Mount Royal University*

Sylvia Perez-Hardy, *Rochester Institute of Technology*

Nelson Piedra, *Universidad Técnica Particular de Loja*

Wayne Pollock, *Hillsborough Community College*

James Pomykalski, *Susquehanna University*

Annu Prabhakar, *University of Cincinnati*

Lakshmi Prayaga, *University of West Florida*

Barbara Price, *Georgia Southern University*

Junfeng Qu, *Clayton State University*

Hugo Rehesaar, *Griffith University*

Han Reichgelt, *Southern Polytechnic State University*

Janet Renwick, *University of Arkansas - Fort Smith*

Dale Rowe, *Brigham Young University*

Rick Gee, *Okanagan College*

Kathy Gill, *University of Washington*

Bryan Goda, *University of Washington*

Mingwei Gong, *Mount Royal University*

Prakash Goteti, *Mahindra Satyam*

Marco Aurélio Graciotto Silva, *University of São Paulo*

Ruth Guthrie, *Cal Poly Pomona*

Shekhar H M P, *Education and Research Department, Infosys Technologies Ltd.*

Thomas Hacker, *Purdue University*

Raymond Hansen, *Purdue University*

Richard Helps, *Brigham Young University*

Gregory Hislop, *Drexel University*

Ricardo Hoar, *Mount Royal University*

Edward Holden, *Rochester Institute of Technology*

Arno Hollosi, *Campus 02 University of Applied Sciences*

William Homer, *Core Business Technology Solutions*

Rick Homkes, *Purdue University*

Janet Hughes, *University of Dundee*

Diane Igoche, *Effat University*

Sudharsan Iyengar, *Winona State University*

R. Kent Jackson, *Brigham Young University - Idaho*

Mark Jaeger, *Baker College*

Hetal Jasani, *Northern Kentucky University*

Michael Jonas, *University of New Hampshire at Manchester*

Harshad Joshi, *Indiana University*

Yih-Ruey Juang, *Jinwen University of Science and Technology*

Suraj Juddoo, *Middlesex University*

Shakeel Khoja, *Institute of Business Administration*

Jane Kochanov, *Penn State Harrisburg*

Steven Kollmansberger, *South Puget Sound Community College*

Walter Kuhn, *University of Applied Sciences for Business Administration Zurich*

Deborah LaBelle, *Nazareth College of Rochester*

Mary Last

Kam Fui Lau, *Armstrong Atlantic State University*

Seamus Lawless, *Trinity College Dublin*

Chi Un Lei, *University of Hong Kong*

Rebecca Rutherford, *Southern Polytechnic State University*

Amber Settle, *DePaul University*

Faezeh Seyedarabi, *City University London*

Zaffar Ahmed Shaikh, *Institute of Business Administration, Karachi*

Carlos Silva, *University of Minho*

Suyash Sinha, *Microsoft Corporation*

Edward Sobiesk, *United States Military Academy*

Theresa Steinbach, *DePaul University*

Adriana Steyn, *University of Pretoria*

Mark Stockman, *University of Cincinnati*

Leigh Ann Sudol-DeLyser, *Carnegie Mellon University*

Andrew Suhy, *University of Michigan*

Bob Sweeney, *University of South Alabama*

Maciej Syslo, *Nicolaus Copernicus University*

Sue Talley, *Capella University*

Suleyman Uludag, *University of Michigan - Flint*

Faith-Michael Uzoka, *Mount Royal University*

Jey Veerasamy, *Baker College Online*

Xinli Wang, *Michigan Technological University*

Janice Warner, *Georgian Court University*

Linda Webster, *Westminster College*

Elissa Weeden, *Rochester Institute of Technology*

Glenn Wilson, *University of Southern Maine*

Jenifer Winter, *University of Hawaii*

James Woolen, *Ferris State University*

Daniel Yoas, *Pennsylvania College of Technology*

Dongqing Yuan, *University of Wisconsin - Stout*

Chi Zhang, *Southern Polytechnic State University*

Stephen Zilora, *Rochester Institute of Technology*

SIGITE/RIIT 2012 Sponsor & Supporters

Sponsor:

Supporters:

Evaluations of AODV and DSR for QoS Requirements

Hetal Jasani, Ph. D.

Department of Computer Science
Northern Kentucky University
Highland Heights, KY, USA, 41099
jasanih1@nku.edu

ABSTRACT

A set of wireless mobile nodes communicate with each other without using any fixed infrastructure in mobile ad hoc network (MANET). MANET devices usually communicate in a seamless manner. There are multiple routing protocols that have been developed for MANETs. There is a need to support VoIP applications in MANETs as they gain popularity and require an efficient routing protocol. Many voice applications have strict requirements such as delay, jitter, etc. This work evaluates the performance of AODV and DSR by comparing the results while supporting VoIP applications with regular HTTP and FTP applications. IEEE 802.11n has been used at link layer for all the nodes and servers in evaluated network. An extensive set of performance experiments with a wide variety of settings has been conducted and findings based on results are concluded for these protocols.

Categories and Subject Descriptors

C.4 [**Computer Systems Organization**]: Performance of Systems, Modeling techniques.

General Terms

Measurement, Performance

Keywords

Modeling and Simulation, AODV, DSR, MANET, OPNET, VoIP

1. INTRODUCTION

Mobile ad hoc networks (MANETs) are created on the fly quickly where infrastructure is not available. All mobile nodes will help each other to forward packets to other mobile nodes in the network that may not be within immediate wireless transmission range of each other. These MANETs are characterized by frequently changing network topology, multi-hop wireless connectivity, and the need for efficient dynamic routing protocols [15]. On-demand routing protocols are widely used because they use much lower routing overhead than proactive protocols [12]. Two most widely studied on-demand ad hoc routing protocols are Ad Hoc on-demand Distance Vector (AODV) [15] and Dynamic Source Routing (DSR) [7, 8]. They both construct and depend on a uni-path route for data communications. They need to initiate a new route discovery process whenever there is a link break on the route. This results in a high routing process overhead. On-

demand multipath routing protocols can alleviate these problems by establishing multiple routes between the source node and destination node during one route discovery process.

Due to the rising popularity of voice over IP (VoIP) applications in the commercial setting, VoIP QoS support in MANETs has become an important area of research. The VoIP QoS requirements generally include high packet delivery ratio, low delay and low jitter while supporting regular web and FTP traffic. This paper presents comparative study results of two MANET routing protocols: AODV and DSR. This research allows us for better understanding of protocols in terms of QoS required by VoIP applications while using IEEE 802.11n [10] at MAC layer.

2. DSR AND AODV

This section provides a quick overview of DSR [3, 7] and AODV [15]. For complete details see the original papers.

2.1 DSR

As name suggest, the Dynamic Source Routing protocol (DSR) is based on the well-known concept of source routing [7, 12]. It is a reactive (on-demand) routing protocol. The protocol includes two major operational components: Route Discovery and Route Maintenance, and three types of route control messages, i.e., Route Request (RREQ), Route Reply (RREP), and Route Error (RERR). When a source node in the mobile ad hoc network attempts to send a packet to a destination but it does not have a route to that destination in its route cache, it initiates a route discovery process by broadcasting a Route Request packet (RREQ). This route request packet contains the source node address, the destination node address, unique sequence number, and an empty route record. Each intermediate node, upon receiving a route request for the first time, will check its own route cache. If it has no route to the destination, the intermediate node will add its own address to the route record and rebroadcast the RREQ. If it has a route to the destination in its route cache, the intermediate node will append the cached route to the route record and initiate a Route Reply (RREP) back to the source node. The RREP contains the complete route record from the source to the destination. The intermediate node ignores the late arrival of the same route request by examining the sequence number. If the node receiving the route request is the destination node, it will copy the route record contained in the route request and send a RREP back to the source. In most simulation implementations, the destination node will reply to all the route requests received, since DSR is capable of caching multiple paths to a certain destination. Also, the replies from the destination reflect the up-to-date routing information the most precisely.

Because of the node movement, the routes discovered may no longer be valid over time. The route maintenance mechanism is accomplished by sending route error packets (RERR). If a link break occurs while the route is active, the node upstream of the break propagates a RERR to the source node to inform it of the unreachable destination(s). Each node, upon receiving the RERR, removes all the routes that contain the broken link from its cache. Consequently, if the source node still desires the route, it can reinitiate route discovery. In DSR, each node transmitting the packet is responsible for confirming that the packet has been received by the next hop along the source route. This can be done by either a link layer acknowledgement (as in IEEE 802.11), or a passive acknowledgement (in which the first transmitting node confirms the receipt at the second node by overhearing the second node transmitting the packet to the third node). It can also be achieved by a DSR-specific software acknowledgement returned by the next hop. Once a route is entered into the cache, the failure of the route can only be detected when it is actually used to transmit a packet but fails to confirm the receipt by the next hop.

2.2 AODV

The Ad-hoc On-demand Distance Vector (AODV) [15] routing algorithm is an on-demand routing protocol for MANET, meaning that it builds routes between nodes only as desired by source nodes. It maintains these routes as long as the source nodes need them. AODV uses sequence numbers to ensure the freshness of routes. It is loop-free, self-starting, and scales to large numbers of mobile nodes.

Similar to DSR, Route Request (RREQ) and Route Reply (RREP) are used to build the routes in MANET. When a source node desires a route to a destination for which it does not already have a route, it broadcasts a RREQ packet across the network. Nodes receiving this packet update their information for the source node and set up backwards pointers to the source node in the route tables. In addition to the source node's IP address, current sequence number, and broadcast ID, the RREQ also contains the most recent sequence number for the destination of which the source node is aware. A node receiving the RREQ may send a RREP if it is either the destination or if it has a route to the destination with corresponding sequence number greater than or equal to that contained in the RREQ. If this is the case, it unicasts a RREP back to the source. Otherwise, it rebroadcasts the RREQ. Nodes keep track of the RREQ's source IP address and broadcast ID. They discard the duplicate or previously received RREQ and do not forward it.

As the RREP propagates back to the source, nodes create forward pointers to the destination. Source node may begin to forward data packets to the destination once it receives the RREP. Source node may update its routing information for that destination and begin using the better route if it later receives a RREP containing a greater sequence number or contains the same sequence number with a smaller hop count. Route would be maintained as long as it remains active. A route is considered active as long as data packets are sent periodically from the source node to the destination along that path. If the source node stops sending data packets, the links will time out and eventually be deleted from the intermediate node routing tables. If a link break occurs while the route is active, the node upstream of the break propagates a route error (RERR) message to the source node to inform it of the unreachable destination(s). After receiving the RERR, if the source node still desires the route, it can reinitiate route Discovery. Because the network nodes are mobile, it is likely that many link breakages along a route will occur during the lifetime of that route. AODV allows, in a timely fashion, mobile nodes to respond to link breakages and changes in network topology.

3. RELATED WORK

Four ad hoc routing protocols including AODV and DSR have been evaluated in [3]. They used 50 node models with similar mobility and traffic scenarios that we used. Packet delivery fraction, number of routing packets and distribution of path lengths were used as performance metrics. An earlier version of AODV was used without the query control optimizations. DSR demonstrated vastly superior routing load performance, and somewhat superior packet delivery and route length performance.

Other papers have compared performance of AODV and DSR including [4]. However, the simulation environment was rather limited, with no link or physical layer models. The routing protocol models also did not include many useful optimizations. This work doesn't consider QoS requirement for real-time applications such as VoIP, video. There are few finding on required QoS in traditional wireless and mobile networks, but they are not complete and suitable for MANETs. Challenges in QoS provisioning is discussed in [9].

In [18], a flexible QoS model for mobile ad-hoc networks (FQMM) is presented, which is a hybrid service model and based on IntServ and Diffserv model. This protocol addresses the basic problem appeared by QoS frameworks [13]. But it cannot solve other problems such as, decision upon traffic classification, allotment of per flow or aggregated service for the given flow, amount of traffic belonging to per flow service, and scheduling or forwarding of the traffic by the intermediate nodes. Reference [11] describes a packet scheduling approach for QoS provisioning in multi-hop wireless networks. Besides the minimum throughput and delay bounds for each flow, the scheduling disciplines seek to achieve fair and maximum allocation of the shared wireless channel bandwidth. The coordination of the adaptation between the different layers of the network in order to solve the problems introduced by scarce and dynamic network resources is described in [2]. Network feedback based on link and acceptable throughput measurements were made to support higher layer and soft quality of service. However, these schemes do not consider the inherent characteristics (changing network topology, limited resource availability, and error-prone shared radio channel) of MANETs and drawbacks of integrated services and differentiated services. In past, researchers have evaluated and compared the performance of AODV, DSR and some other routing protocols. However, they have not studied QoS parameters. Even recently, there are some attempts to evaluate the performance of AODV and DSR and compare the performance parameters [6, 17]. Both have not considered the QoS parameters such as Voice jitter, Voice End-to-End Delay. Another group of researchers [16] has evaluated ZRP (Zonal Routing Protocol) for MANETs using QualNet. They have only considered throughput, end-to-end delay and total bytes received as parameters to compare ZRP with AODV and DSR. Author has evaluated QoS parameters and compared the results in AODV and DSR while using 802.11b at MAC layer with and without 802.11e default setting in OPNET [5]. In this paper, VoIP applications (including web and FTP) performance has been evaluated while using 802.11n at MAC layer. Authors have also evaluated VoIP performance in WLAN [1, 14]. However, they didn't evaluate MANET routing protocols as they focus on WLAN technology.

4. PERFORMANCE METRICS

We carry out the performance evaluation of the two ad hoc routing protocols, AOVD and DSR, to determine which is more efficient in different network settings including real-time application such as VoIP. We have used OPNET Modeler to model ad hoc network containing the nodes using the DSR and AODV for separate scenarios. A variety of network settings variations including changes in topology, application traffic, node mobility have been evaluated. The main network parameters for QoS performance that compared are: voice jitter, voice end-to-end delay, voice throughput, HTTP object response time, number of packets dropped, etc.

5. PERFORMANCE EVALUATIONS

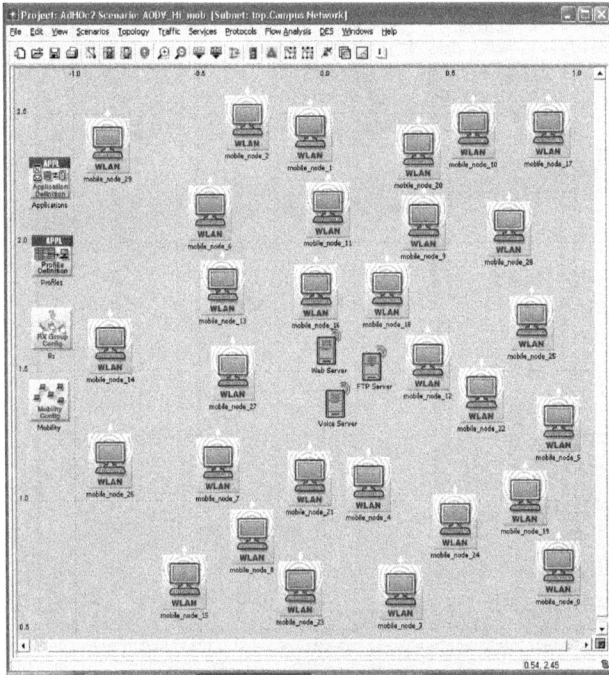

Figure 1. Network Setup

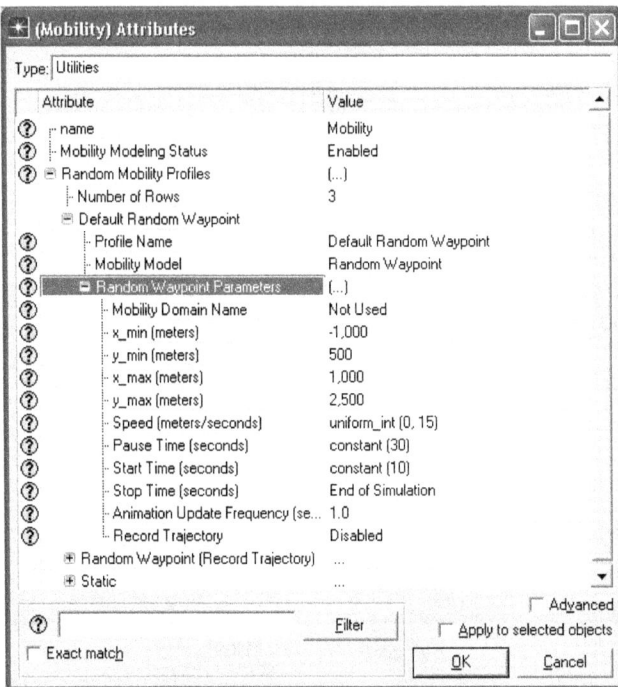

Figure 2. Mobility Profile Configuration

The OPNET network topology that used to evaluate the performance of DSR and AODV ad-hoc routing protocols is shown in Figure 1. The topology of the network is generated by randomly distributing 30 nodes in a region of 2 km x 2 km area. In OPNET Modeler, mobility, applications and profiles have been configured such that all nodes generate FTP, HTTP and VoIP application traffic.

Two simulations are run using DSR and AODV respectively with same amount of application traffic, same amount mobility and all other same settings. Mobility includes the nodes moving from 0 to 15 meters per second. All nodes including MANET workstations and servers use 802.11n at MAC layer with default parameters.

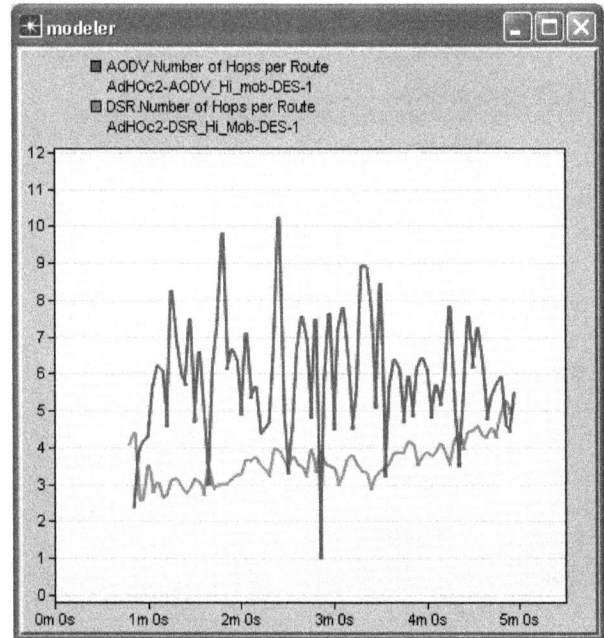

Figure 3. Number of Hops

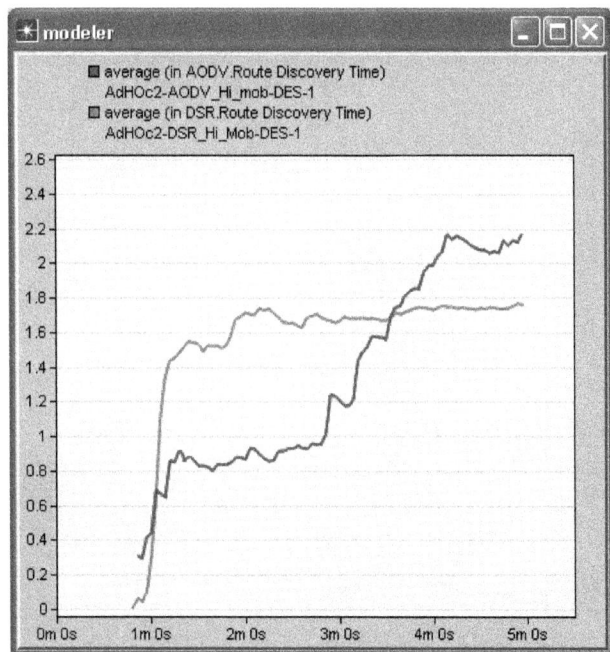

Figure 4. Route Discovery Time

3

Figure 3, 4 5 and 6 show the result comparisons of two simulation scenarios for AODV and DSR routing protocol related data (i.e., number of hops, route discovery time, routing traffic sent, total routing errors sent). Route discovery time in Figure 4 is higher for DSR from beginning and stays at same level. However, AODV route discovery time increases as simulation progresses. This is due to the nature of DSR and AODV. In DSR, intermediate nodes will keep the routes in their cache while AODV doesn't use caching mechanism. Due to the same reason, number of hops is much lower in DSR as shown in Figure 3. As shown in Figure 5, total routing traffic sent is much lower in AODV than DSR. Figure 6 shows the total number of routing errors sent are lower in AODV than DSR.

Remaining results focus on application performance especially VoIP application. Important parameter in MANETs to end-users is end-to-end delay. Delay is caused and altered by many factors. Some of the factors include size of network, movement, and data transfer type. Figure 7 indicates voice traffic end-to-end (i.e., application level) delay. DSR has a larger amount of delay as it caches the route and stale route may be used. There will be errors, and retransmissions due to the use of stale routes from the cache. In AODV, the routes are made on demand and allow for better route selection while considering the current topology which decreases the voice end to end delay.

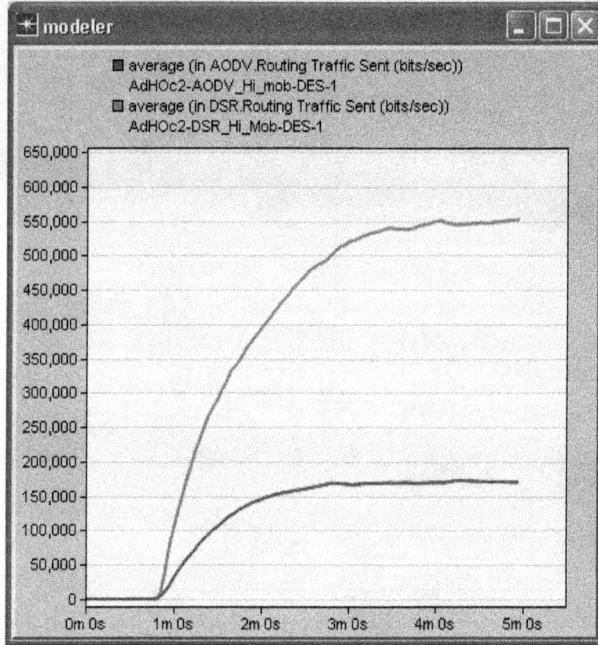

Figure 5. Routing Traffic Sent

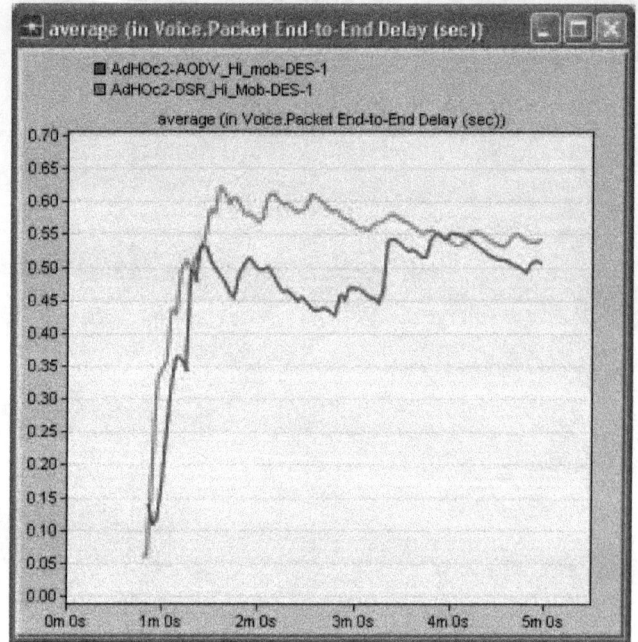

Figure 7. Voice End-to-End Delay

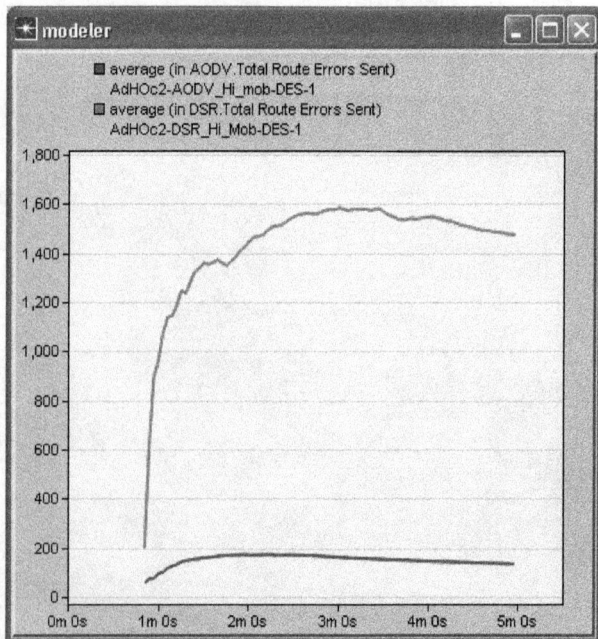

Figure 6. Total Routing Errors Sent

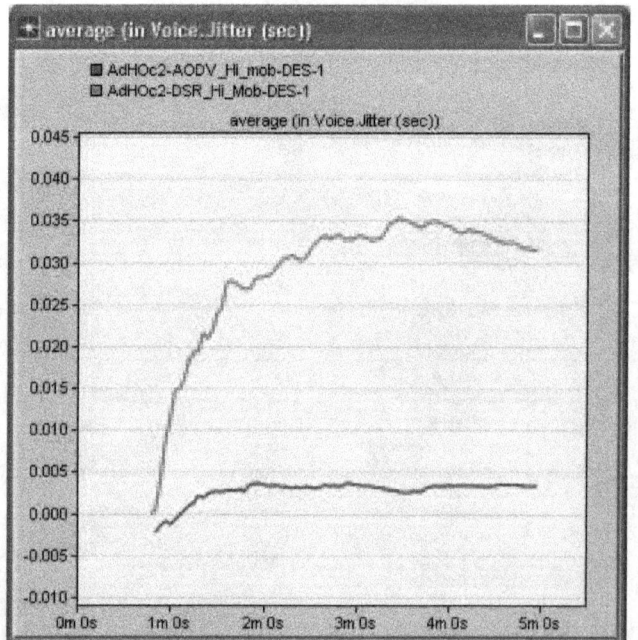

Figure 8. Voice Jitter

Figure 8 shows the voice traffic jitter comparison of AODV with DSR. Jitter plays an important role in VoIP quality of service.

Jitter is a measurement of the variability over time of the packet latency across a network. If two consecutive packets leave the source node with time stamps t1 & t2 and are played back at the destination node at time t3 & t4, then: Jitter = (t4 - t3) - (t2 - t1). AODV has overall less jitter because it creates new routes and not using the same route that may become crowed or congested. DSR has an increasing rate due to the fact that more nodes may use the cached stale routes.

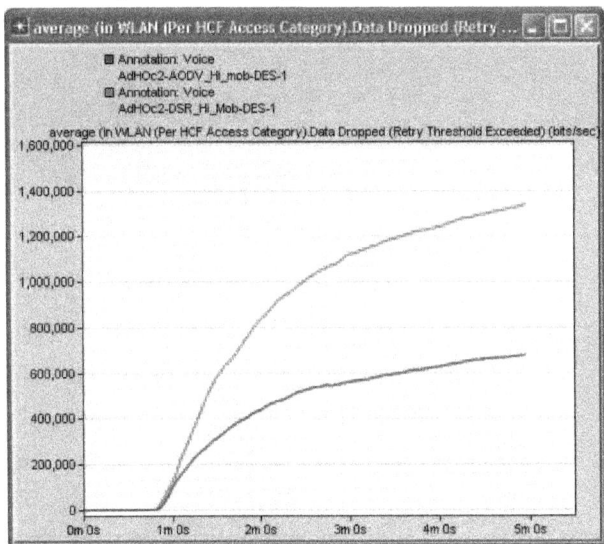

Figure 9. Data Dropped (Buffer Overflow)

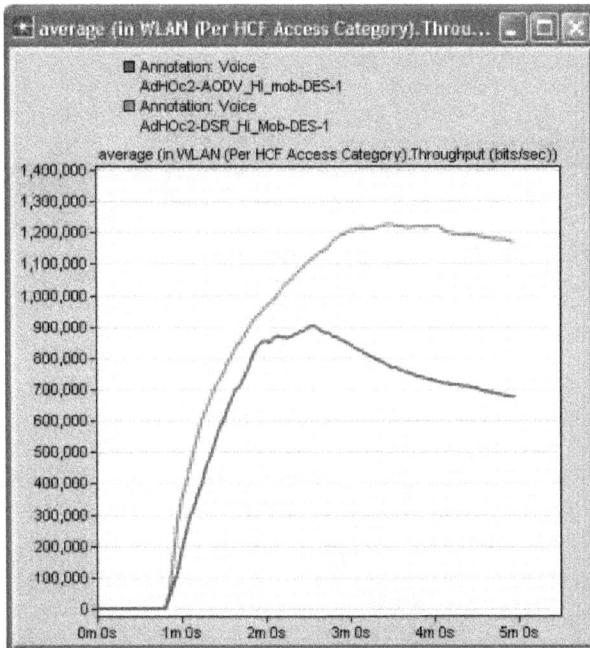

Figure 10. Data Dropped (Max Retransmissions)

Figure 9 and Figure 10 show the voice data dropped due to buffer overflow and retransmissions respectively. Figure 9 shows the total higher layer voice traffic (in bits/sec) dropped by all the 802.11e-capable WLAN MACs in the network due to either having the full higher layer voice buffer, or the size of the voice packet, which is greater than the maximum allowed data size defined in the IEEE 802.11 standard. Figure 10 indicates the total higher layer voice traffic (in bits/sec) dropped by all the 802.11e-capable WLAN MACs in the network due to consistently failing retransmissions. This statistic reports the number of the voice packets that are discarded because the MAC couldn't receive any

ACKs for the (re)transmissions of those packets or their fragments, and the packets' retry counts reached the MAC's retry limit.

As IEEE 802.11n used with 802.11e default settings, voice has higher priority than HTTP and FTP traffic. Voice traffic has a user priority level of 6 (i.e., interactive voice) while HTTP and FTP traffic has the user priority level of 0 (i.e., best effort). Due to the priority and nature of AODV and DSR, DSR has higher number of voice packets dropped due to buffer overflow and after maximum number of retransmissions.

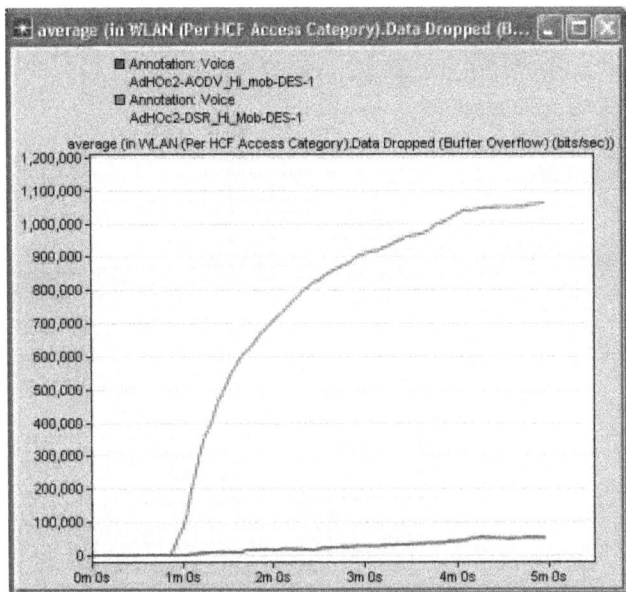

Figure 11. Voice Throughput

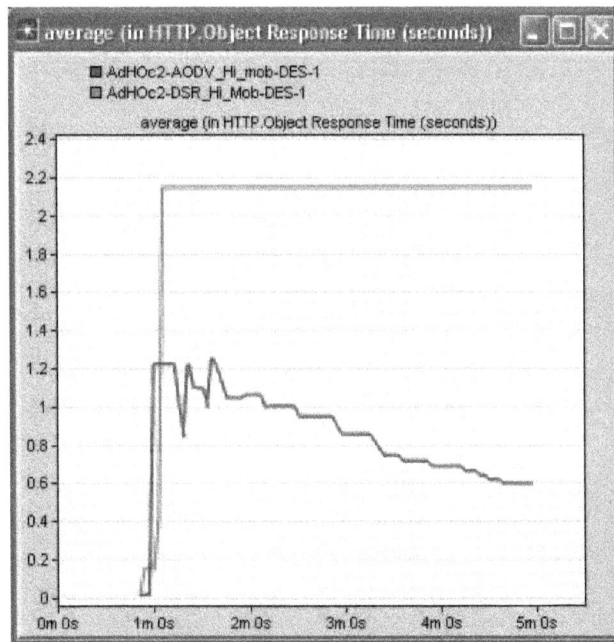

Figure 12. HTTP Object Response Time

Figure 11 shows the voice throughput for both scenarios. This indicates the total voice traffic in bits/sec, successfully received and forwarded to the higher layer by all the 802.11e-capable WLAN MACs in the network. DSR has higher voice throughput than AODV.

Figure 12 shows the HTTP object response time response time for comparing AODV and DSR scenarios. Again, AODV seems to work better for HTTP object response time during the simulation as AODV has lower (almost half) time than DSR.

The comparisons of above results show that AODV is more efficient than that of DSR in various aspects. In situations that require voice data, AODV would be recommended while using IEEE 802.11n at MAC layer.

6. CONCLUSIONS

DSR and AODV have been evaluated for voice traffic while using IEEE 802.11n at MAC layer. OPNET has been used to facilitate the simulation of real world scenarios. FTP, HTTP and VoIP traffic have been incorporated into the network using application and profile configuration. High mobility of mobile nodes has been configured using mobility configuration in OPNET. One scenario for As a result of creating simulations for both Dynamic Source Routing and Ad hoc On Demand Distance Vector, the study is able to capture data for a comparison. By looking at the results, AODV would be the choice of protocol to use in most if not all situations especially when voice traffic is more important. There was significant performance gain with lower delays, jitter, and number of dropped packets. Voice is a vital part of the network such as disaster recovery. In relatively small ad-hoc networks with regular traffic and high mobility, AODV would be the better choice of routing protocol for voice traffic.

7. ACKNOWLEDGMENTS

The author would also like to give an extended acknowledgment to the OPNET for allowing the use of their OPNET Modeler software for educational advancement at Northern Kentucky University.

8. REFERENCES

[1] Anand, G.C.S.; Vaidya, R.R.; Velmurugan, T., Performance Analysis of VoIP Traffic using various Protocols and Throughput enhancement in WLANs, *Proceeding of International Conference on Computer, Communication and Electrical Technology (ICCCET)*, 2011, pp. 176 – 180.

[2] Bharghavan, V., Lee, K., Lu, S., Ha, S., Li, J. R., Dwyer, D., The Timely Adaptive Resource Management Architecture, *IEEE Personal Communication Magazine*, Vol. 5, No.8, August 1998, pp. 20-31.

[3] Broch, J., Maltz, D. A., Johnson, D. B., Hu, Y.-C., and Jetcheva, J.G., A performance comparison of multi-hop wireless ad hoc network routing protocols, *In Proceeding of the 4th international Conference on Mobile Computing and Networking*, pages 85-97, October 1998.

[4] Das, S. R., Castaneda, R., Yan, J., and Sengupta, R., Comparative performance evaluation of routing protocols for mobile ad hoc networks, *In 7th International Conference on Computer communications and Networking*, pages 153-161, October 1998.

[5] Jasani, H., Quality of Service Evaluations of Mobile Ad-Hoc Routing Protocols, *5th International Conference and Exhibition on Next Generation Mobile Applications, Services, and Technologies*, NGMAST 2011, Cardiff, Wales, UK, pp. 123-128, Sept. 14-16, 2011.

[6] Jayakumar, G. and Ganapathy, G., Performance Comparison of Mobile Ad-hoc Network Routing Protocol, *International Journal of Computer Science and Network Security* (IJCSNS), Vol.7 No.11, pp. 77-84 November 2007.

[7] Johnson, D. B., Maltz, D. A., and Broch, J., DSR: The Dynamic Source Routing Protocol for Multi-Hop Wireless Ad Hoc Networks. in Ad Hoc Networking, chapter 5, pp. 139–172, *Addison-Wesley*, 2001.

[8] Johnson, D. B., Maltz, D. A., Hu, Y.-C., and Jetcheva, J.G., The Dynamic Source Routing Protocol for Mobile Ad Hoc Networks, IETF Internet draft draft-ietf-manet-dsr-06.txt, November 2001.

[9] Karimi, M., Pan, D., Challenges for Quality of Service (QoS) in Mobile Ad-hoc Networks (MANETs), *Wireless and Microwave Technology Conference*, 2009. IEEE 10th Annual, pp.1-5, April 2009.

[10] Lakshmanan, S.; Jeongkeun Lee; Etkin, R.; Sung-Ju Lee; Sivakumar, R., Realizing high performance multi-radio 802.11n wireless networks, *Proceeding of 8th Annual IEEE Communications Society Conference on Sensor, Mesh and Ad Hoc Communications and Networks (SECON)*, 2011, pp. 242 - 250

[11] Luo, H., Lu, S. , Bharghavan, V., Cheng, L., and Zhong, G., A Packet Scheduling Approach to QoS Support in Multi-hop Wireless Networks, *Mobile Networks and Applications* Vol. 9, Issue 3, 2004, pp. 193-206.

[12] Maltz, D. A., Broch, J., Jetcheva, J.G., and Johnson, D. B., The Effects of On-Demand Behavior in Routing Protocols for Multi-Hop Wireless Ad Hoc Networks, *IEEE Journal on Selected Areas in Communications*, vol. 17, no. 8, pp. 1439-1453, August 1999.

[13] Murthy C. S. R., Manoj, B. S., Ad-hoc Wireless Networks Architectures and Protocols, *Prentice Hall*, Upper Saddle River, NJ 07458, 2004.

[14] Neupane, K., Elam, A., Kulgachev, V., Vasireddy, S., Jasani, H., "Measuring the performance of VoIP over Wireless LAN", ACM SIGITE 2011 Conference on Information Technology Education, Oct. 20-22, 2011.

[15] Perkins, C. E., Royer E. M., and Das, S. R., Performance Comparison of Two On-Demand Routing Protocols for Ad Hoc Networks, *IEEE Personal Communications*, Feb 2001.

[16] Raju, S. R. Runkana, K., Mungara, J., Performance measurement and analysis of ZRP for MANETs using network simulator-QualNet, *Wireless Information Technology and Systems (ICWITS)*, 2010 IEEE International Conference on, pp.1-4, Aug. 28 2010-Sept. 3 2010.

[17] Sharma, N., Rana, S., Sharma, R. M.,"Provisioning of Quality of Service in MANETs performance analysis & comparison (AODV and DSR)," Computer Engineering and Technology (ICCET), 2010 2nd International Conference on , vol.7, no., pp.V7-243-V7-248, 16-18 April 2010.

[18] Xiao, H., Seah, W.G., Lo, A., and Chua, K.C., A Flexible Quality of Service Model for Mobile Ad-hoc Networks (FQMM), *In Proceedings of IEEE Vehicular Technology Conference* (VTC 2000-Fall), Vol. 1,No.4, May 2000, pp.397-413.

Mapping the Cyber Security Terrain in a Research Context

Dale C. Rowe Ph.D.
Brigham Young University
Information Technology Program
Provo, UT, 84602
1 (801) 422 6051

dale_rowe@byu.edu

Barry Lunt Ph.D.
Brigham Young University
Information Technology Program
Provo, UT, 84602
1 (801) 422 2264

luntb@byu.edu

ABSTRACT
In this paper we present a mapping of cyber-security research to information technology as a technical research discipline. We first discuss the evolution of IT as an academic discipline and use this to establish technical research objectives in an IT context. We then present our definition of cyber-security and a proposed research agenda based on these objectives and conclude with a discussion of current projects within our institution.

Categories and Subject Descriptors
C.2.0 [**Computer-Communication Networks**]: General --- Security and Protection.

General Terms
Security

Keywords
Cybersecurity, Information assurance and security, Research, Information technology.

1. INTRODUCTION
In the first two sections of this paper we attempt to identify key research goals that constitute technical information technology research. From here, the discussion will move to focus on cyber-security and specific elements within this domain.

Information Technology is a relatively young discipline, officially recognized by ABET accreditations in 2003. Since this date, there have been many productive efforts to further explore the relationships and interactions between computing programs [7, 13] (also Figure 1). This work has been fruitful in quantifiably identifying the characteristics of an Information Technology program. Indeed, a current project that leverages this knowledge is underway to identify computing program proximity to the IT curriculum throughout the United States [10].

We could compare the evolutionary process of establishing and understanding IT as an academic discipline to an infant's growth and maturation. When an infant is born, the majority of a parent's time with the child is spent in providing nourishment, a warm environment, rudimentary education and other essential life-sustaining provisions. When the new addition to the family has older siblings, there may be brief periods of resentment of the

younger kin. This may be due to the time demands of the infant on their parents. Over time, as the family adjusts there is an increase of support, understanding and love from both parents and siblings.

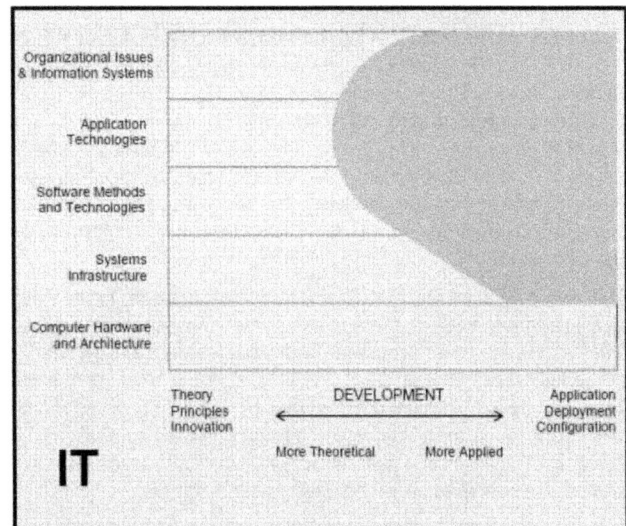

Figure 1 - The IT Fit (CC2005)

When Information Technology was 'born', the question had to be asked 'why'. What need justified a new program, different from all the current computing programs? Some academics viewed the entire concept as preposterous - the very idea that a computing topic wasn't covered in their programs bordered on the offensive (don't you have enough kids already?). Others were apprehensive, perhaps asking the question "what effect would this new program have on current curricula?" (Will you love me any less?). Finally, there were the visionaries who saw the insatiable call for an applied approach to computing as a service-oriented discipline. Thanks to their efforts, IT is now accepted and even on occasion applauded as an academic discipline. Those who before were offended or apprehensive have for the most part grown to respect IT programs and in some instances, even enjoy the fruits of interdisciplinary collaboration such as course sharing. The computing family has grown, and everyone stands to benefit.

Hence although young, IT has reached a recognized level of maturity at least within the educational domain. The very concept of a new conference dedicated to IT research shows a desire to take the discipline a step further (Figure 2), to the next level and poses the question "what constitutes IT research?" Indeed this is a question we have asked among our institution's faculty over the past few years. What is IT research and how does it differ from other computing research agendas?

Permission to make digital or hard copies of all or part of this work for personal or classroom use is granted without fee provided that copies are not made or distributed for profit or commercial advantage and that copies bear this notice and the full citation on the first page. To copy otherwise, or republish, to post on servers or to redistribute to lists, requires prior specific permission and/or a fee.
RIIT'12, October 11–13, 2012, Calgary, Alberta, Canada.
Copyright 2012 ACM 978-1-4503-1643-9/12/10...$15.00.

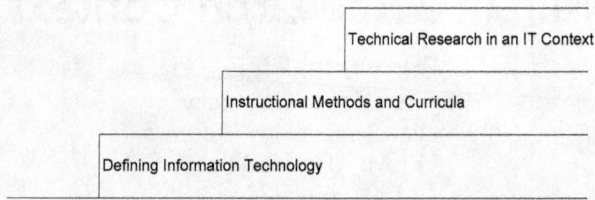

Figure 2 - Evolution of IT Research

Care should be taken when discussing technical research that it is not placed in greater esteem than the preceding steps. The placement of technical research is designed to show how these are necessary pre-requisite steps to understanding IT research and its placement within computing research agendas.

2. TECHNCIAL RESEARCH OBJECTIVES

To say that IT technical research starts today would be presumptuous. There are numerous examples of research papers and funded projects that fall within the IT space. However, it would be fair to say that typically these papers do not self-classify as IT. Papers that purport to be IT tend to focus on the educational topics discussed in the preceding section. Instructional methods, curricula development and standardization have been and will continue to be active research areas.

Yet this year sees the first Research In Information Technology (RIIT) conference to complement the longstanding Special Interest Group in Information Technology Education (SIGITE) conference held annually. If SIGITE is home to these current research areas, what is the purpose of RIIT and what would constitute "good form" for research to take? If the emphasis is on "technical" research more than "instructional" research, how should this complement existing research disciplines?

In a recent experience, one of the authors was asked the question many readers will have heard before. "So what is the difference between IT and Computer Science (CS)?" The individual asking the question was a potential freshman student for a mechanical engineering program but was investigating other programs of interest. Although this author was certain that a complete, accurate response could have been provided in the 139 pages of the IT Model Curriculum [6] he elected to respond as follows.

'What do you thinking computing is all about?'

- 'Programming'

'Programming is a big part of CS and IT, so let's look at that. In CS we focus on understanding the relationship between the software program, and the computer system. If the person using that program doesn't 'get' it, or understand it, then they need training so that they can. In IT we focus on the relationship between the computer system and the end-user. If the user doesn't 'get it', then in IT, we would consider that a failure of the system, not necessarily the user.'

Although slightly anecdotal, we believe this goes a long way in identifying a key characteristic of IT. IT is a service-oriented discipline. The IT professional should be a user advocate, an intermediary catalyst between the user and whatever computing technology is being used. We propose that technical IT research should follow a similar route in being (see also Figure 3):

- Applicable (capable of being applied)
- Systems & Service-Oriented
- Usable

We posed the question 'In as few words as possible, please describe IT research' to department faculty, computer support representatives, and institutional IT faculty. We then categorized responses into the above list. Interestingly there is a close correlation with Agresti's list of challenges facing IT professionals which include [1] (parenthesis added):

1. Create effective configurations and productive platforms from the array of existing products and services. (Applicable, Services)

2. Address the myriad practical issues surrounding people and technology coming together. (Systems)

3. Establish nonburdensome policies and practices so the technology is maximally accessible, usable and effective for people to do their jobs, while being secure and reliable at the same time. (Usable)

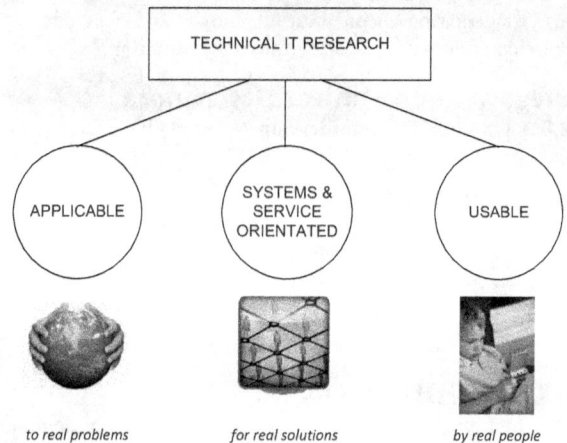

Figure 3 - IT Technical Research Objectives

This correlation indicates a positive direction. By using recognized concerns for IT professionals as key research criteria there is a natural alignment with the instructional domain of IT in user advocacy and service provisioning.

2.1 Applicable Research

This term may be somewhat ambiguous with 'being applicable to IT' so we have attached the additional explanation 'capable of being applied'. IT research should be capable of being applied by design. Ideally it should attempt to answer a real-world problem and provide a practical, implementable solution (a real answer). Some may argue that this is not true science in the traditional sense of hypothetical theorem and proof/disprove and they would be correct. This approach bears much greater resemblance to the engineering methodology and seems fitting to the service-oriented nature of IT. For this reason we propose it as a key identifying attribute of IT research.

2.2 Systems & Service-Oriented

Systems orientation refers to emphasizing the system rather than individual components. When asked to describe IT, Mark Bailey, IT Lab Manager, responded that *'IT focuses on designing, building and maintaining secure interfaces to integrate systems and deliver reliable services'*. This is a precise and eloquent definition of the IT systems approach.

Service-oriented refers to the provisioning of a service to a user or users. This is quite different from systems-oriented and one may rightly question why they are amalgamated in this discussion. To offer the simplest possible explanation, service-orientation is the 'what' and 'why', whereas systems-orientation refers to the 'how'.

The world we live in is an interconnected socio-technical system of systems. A motherboard under a magnifying glass can show capacitors, resistors and circuits. Now imagine the magnifying glass slowly zooming out bringing first the entire board, then computer into vision. Continuing to zoom out, a series of interconnected computers and users is now in view, and then a corporate network within a building. If this process is continued ad-infinitum, organizations, individuals, governments, citizens and all technology can be viewed as a single, if extremely complex system of systems.

To serve, or provide services to this community, IT must understand the system context. An IT professional understands a systems purpose and function, and how components interface and work together to provide this. The ability to analyze a system and decompose it to a lower level to identify interfaces is a key principle of systems engineering. At this level, design, implementation and problem finding can take place. Each component can typically be seen as its own system and can undergo a similar iterative process. Once the interface work completes, components can be validated, assembled and (re)integrated [16].

IT by definition is a systems service-oriented discipline and we list this as a key indicator for IT research.

2.3 Usable

As referenced in the anecdotal professor to prospective student conversation and reinforced in the third challenge facing IT professionals, usability is a core differentiator for IT. The significance of systems being usable for the non-technically savvy sets IT apart from all other computing disciplines. IT is concerned with the sociological impact of technology and how technology can support and sustain everyday productivity and lifestyle. Computing technology should enrich rather than weaken, enhance rather than diminish and enlighten rather than confuse.

IT research likewise should consider the usability aspects of innovation and emphasize this over pure algorithmic elegance.

3. THE CYBER-SECURITY TERRAIN

With research objectives clearly laid out, the focus may now be turned to discuss a specific subset of IT research, namely cyber-security. Cyber-security is one of the most discussed IT topics in recent years yet does not form one of the five 'pillars' of IT [6]. Rather it acts as a overlaying structure, connecting and binding all bodies of knowledge and forming an intricate thread between them [12] as shown in Figure 4.

There can be confusion between the term 'Information Assurance and Security' (IAS) and 'Cyber Security. While we note many similarities between these terms, we believe there is a key differentiating factor that is more than a simple re-branding [2]. In a traditional IAS context, the primary word is information. IAS is concerned with the confidentiality, integrity and availability of information. Although the characteristics of information have been expanded to include authentication and non-repudiation [8], the focus remains on information.

In contrast the term cyber-security reflects the relationships and interconnections between cyberspace and the physical world. While information is certainly a key element in this relationship,

the focus is on the security of cyber-systems, minimizing the risk of unintended cyber-events particularly in the context of those that have a cyber-to-physical domain effect and responding to such events [11]. As cyber-security encompasses IAS in this context, it can be said that cyber-security is both a rebranding, and scope change of IAS (Figure 5).

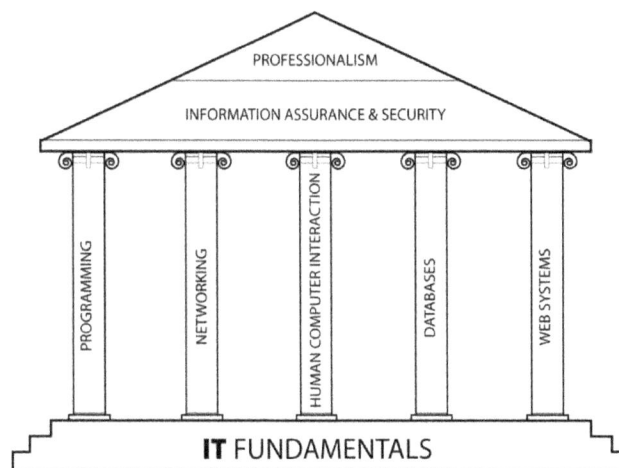

Figure 4 - The IT Body of Knowledge (IT2008)

Previously we have justified how IT provides a best-fit to cyber-security in an instructional context [12]. Likewise there are unique benefits to conducting cyber-security research in an information technology context. The application of research in this manner presents a significant difference both in the objectives and methodology from traditional computing research along with distinct advantages that are not found elsewhere.

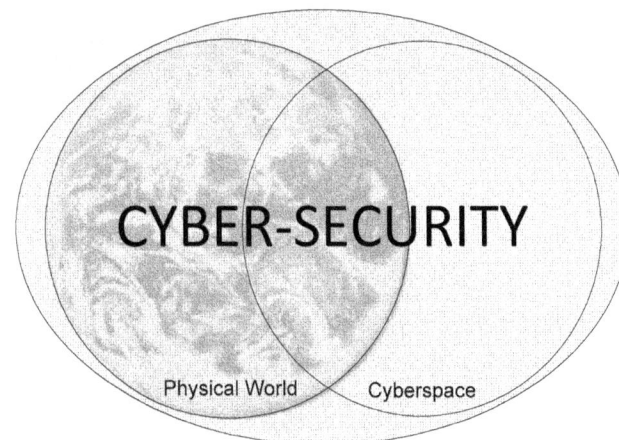

Figure 5 - Cyber Security Terrain

3.1 Applicability (Working with Industry)

One of the unique attributes of information technology is its growth on top of an established profession. Information technology professionals were around before IT degrees. The establishment of IT as an academic discipline has involved, for a significant part, an effort to identify the skills and knowledge held by these professionals [10].

From this background, IT has a rather special relationship with industry. Not only are many IT programs based on the initial study of IT professionals, they seek to maintain proximity to current industry needs. Within our own program we solicit feedback from students, the ABET accreditation process, the NSA/DHS Center of Academic Excellence evaluation process and an Industry Advisory Board (IAB) panel to keep the program up-to-date with industry needs.

It would make sense then, in a research context, to continue what has been a successful partnership. The reader may have already noticed that the graphics and italic text located in the lower half of Figure 3 are not typical of an academic publication. Indeed these may be more at home in an organization's public relations media. However their use here is deliberate and to illustrate a specific point: *IT programs understand the industry profession, and industry professionals can relate to IT programs.* This mutual comprehension presents a great window of opportunity for collaboration in finding research projects that will provide solutions to today's security concerns.

This is not to say that IT research should be a 'hired gun' to solve organizational issues (this is a job for graduating students!). Faculty should be particularly cautious to carefully consider research opportunities for both their intellectual merit and broader impact. Research questions shared by, or that will benefit multiple organizations, can be good indicators of a project's potential impact.

3.2 Systems and Service-Oriented

Research over recent years has highlighted the importance of security across the curriculum [11, 12][3–5, 15]. The placement of security in such a manner provides students with an applied awareness of security throughout their studies. This is an excellent foundation from which to extend research.

Today, most security vulnerabilities stem from a lack of awareness during a system's development. A professional programmer may have neglected to sanitize inputs on an application, a home run e-commerce business may transmit sensitive information using HTTP GET instead of POST requests, or an organization might not filter e-mails based on sender reputation and open a malicious spear-phishing PDF document sent from an impersonated source.

Security awareness embedded in the core curriculum aims to minimize these mistakes by not only teaching awareness, but equipping students with the skills and knowledge to find better alternatives. This intuitively encourages a systems-approach to service provisioning. Analyzing interfaces at various levels of system analysis provides insight into potential security weaknesses and their system-wide impact.

Placing cyber-security research in a system's and service-oriented context is in alignment with this instructional approach. Security research can be approached with the objective of securely providing a specific technical service or capability. The analysis of the topic can then follow a structured process of decomposition, interface & component analysis and integration. This approach can apply to a process, design, concept or product as required.

3.3 Usability

The term usability is used often in security. Often security and usability are seen at opposite ends of the same spectrum, with each pulling the other in opposing directions. IT strives to balance these by promoting non-intrusive security to achieve optimal functionality. This balancing effort is often perceived to be more art than exact science. Indeed an effort to quantify this relationship may in itself constitute a research project! In a simpler model, the goal of usability is supportive of application

and service orientation. Technology must be usable to be used. The success of the iPhone in bringing smartphones to a non-corporate consumer audience demonstrates that systems which are usable, intuitive and unobtrusive are popular with users.

Thus security research should factor usability into consideration when making assertions or assumptions. It may be well to block all corporate traffic from countries known to be active in malware development; however when a user needs to access a site for legitimate purposes and cannot, he may take a corporate laptop to an alternate location, benefit from a less restrictive internet access policy, subsequently become infected in browsing other sites and bring the infection back within his organization's security perimeter. Surely the organization is part to blame in restricting the employees ability to conduct his job? Would it not be better to design a system that filters only malicious data?

Although this is a greatly simplified illustration, it highlights the importance of usability in security research. Cyber security research should strive to incorporate usability as a key feature in determining a systems overall security posture.

4. RESEARCH PROJECTS

With these criteria applied in the context of cyber-security it is fitting to discuss specific research projects in the same manner. This is not intended to be a detailed project analysis, but rather a high-level overview that illustrates how a specific research effort can benefit from aligning itself to these three goals.

4.1 Critical Infrastructure Protection (CIP)

Critical cyber infrastructure refers to computer-controlled industrial processes providing essential services. These services can include water, electricity, fuel, transportation and shelter. There are several security concerns among these services which include:

- Aging legacy infrastructure
- Lack of standardization
- Internet connectivity
- Real-time industrial processes
- Lack of security awareness among ICS[1] designers and operators
- Lack of ICS awareness among computing professionals.

While it may seem a stretch to have such a vast topic defined as a research project, it places well within the parameters previously discussed. In order to provide effective security the system must be viewed holistically, decomposed to its component interfaces and analyzed at each level. Several subprojects at our own institution deal with specific concerns such as anomaly based intrusion detection, SCADA forensics, and embedded security device intelligence (ESDI).

These projects are each excellent examples of IT research projects. They have applicability to real-world problems, are heavily systems and service-oriented, and have real-world usability as a key measurement of success. It should be noted that projects are not necessarily constrained to a single IT body of knowledge topic (or pillar), but can (and often should) span multiple topics. In this example, programming, networking, HCI, databases and web systems are all key elements.

---

[1] ICS refers to Industrial Control Systems, a term given to the computer control of industrial processes.

4.2 Multi-User Computer Aided Applications (v-CAx)

This project is a collaborative effort between multiple institutions and programs as part of an NSF I/UCRC Center for e-Design. It stands for new (nu) computer-aided applications that are truly collaborative. The concept is to transition current single-user CAD architectures to multi-user where several users can simultaneously modify CAx models, including assemblies [9].

The cyber-security research is a subproject within this center that is designing and providing the security architecture for this system. A team of students are analyzing requirements to build a security model and identify potential vulnerabilities. The production of CAx products that support simultaneous access from multiple users has some interesting security concerns. For example, outside of the immediate questions of authentication and access-control, how should a CAD design which contains components of differing sensitivity and knowledge areas be managed in this environment?

This is another example of an applied research project. However in this instance, the research itself is being provided as a service to another department. We have seen that in many IT research areas, this is a common trend.

4.3 The Open Source Cyber Intelligence and Analysis Project (CIAP)

CIAP is a Cyber-Security Forum Initiative (CSFI) project that analyzes the acquisition of raw intelligence data from the public domain and the process by which it can become actionable intelligence. In particular it discusses processes of verification and classification to give information a quantifiable measure of confidence. Rather than being built as a technical platform, it is designed as an operations framework to which both procedures and technical systems may conform.

The project is applicable in the sense that the framework is a tangible, usable set of procedures. It is systems-oriented in its analysis of data and calculations of confidence, and service-oriented in its purpose. The framework itself must be simple, concise and functional in order to be usable.

This project differs from others in that there is no direct technical deliverable. However, IT research is also well-suited to creating such frameworks and methods and there are numerous other cases of this. (ITIL, Security Awareness Programs, Pentesting Frameworks).

4.4 Other Project Concepts

As can be seen, the cyber-security research domain in IT is rich and diverse. The goals which have been outlined in this paper lend themselves to a variety of real issues worthy of investigation. Other potential areas include (but are not limited to):

- Embedded and mobile computing
- Organizational security
- Incident response
- Compliance and auditing
- System hardening
- Infrastructure architecture
- Exploit and malware propagation analysis

5. CONCLUSIONS

In this paper we have discussed the evolution of IT research as a technical field and how the IT model curriculum lends itself to technical research. We have presented three criteria which we have found to be effective indicators of IT research and applied these to the cyber-security domain.

It can be seen that IT technical research naturally self-positions a much needed space and complements existing research agendas such as computer-science and computer-engineering. In many instances, IT research can become an effective bridge between these disciplines [14] and can help the flow of security awareness between different domains and vernaculars.

Due to the applied nature of, and demand for IT research, extra care should be sought in project selection to ensure the intellectual merit and broader impact justify the choice of project. We believe this a key element to gaining acceptance in other computing disciplines as a respected, valid and equal research discipline.

In conclusion we invite further discussion of IT research as a technical research discipline and are particularly interested in feedback within the cyber-security space. We also acknowledge and are grateful for the efforts of others in helping promote IT as a needed critical research discipline.

6. REFERENCES

[1] Agresti, W. 2011. Toward an IT Agenda. *Communications of the Association for Information Systems*. 28, 1 (2011), Article 17.

[2] Agresti, W.W. 2010. The Four Forces Shaping Cybersecurity. *IEEE Computer*. 43, 2 (2010), 101–104.

[3] Dark, M. 2006. Implementation of Information Assurance and Security in Existing IT Curricula. (2006).

[4] Dark, M.J. et al. 2006. Integrating Information Assurance and Security into IT Education: A Look at the Model Curriculum and Emerging Practice. *Journal of Information Technology Education*. 5, (2006), 389–403.

[5] Irvine, C.E. et al. 1998. Integrating Security into the Curriculum. *IEEE Computer*. 31, 12 (1998), 25–30.

[6] Lunt, B.M. et al. 2008. Information Technology 2008 - Curriculum Guidelines for Undergraduate Degree Programs in Information Technology. (2008).

[7] Lunt, B.M. et al. 2008. *Information Technology 2008: Curriculum Guidelines for Undergraduate Degree Programs in Information Technology*. Association for Computing Machinery (ACM); IEEE Computer Society.

[8] Maconachy, V.W. et al. 2001. A Model for Information Assurance: An Integrated Approach. *Proceedings of the 2001 IEEE Workshop on Information Assurance and Security* (US Military Academy, West Point, NY, 2001), 11–15.

[9] Red, E. et al. Multi-user architectures for computer-aided engineering collaboration.

[10] Rowe, D.C. et al. 2011. An assessment framework for identifying information technology programs. *ACM SIGITE 2011* (New York, 2011).

[11] Rowe, D.C. et al. 2012. Cyber-Security, IAS and the Cyber Warrior. *The Colloquium for Information Systems Security Education* (Lake Buena Vista, Fl, 2012).

[12] Rowe, D.C. et al. 2011. The Role of Cyber Security in Information Technology. *ACM SIGITE 2011* (New York, 2011).

[13] Shackelford, R. et al. 2005. Computing Curricula 2005: The Overview Report. *Joint Task Force for Computing Curricula 2005*. (2005).

[14] Sheen, F.J. et al. 2012. Large Scale, Real-Time Systems Security Analysis in Higher Education. *American Society of Engineering Education Conference* (San Antonio, Tx, 2012).

[15] White, G. and Nordstrom, G. 1996. Security Across the Curriculum: Using Computer Security to Teach Computer Science Principles. *National Information Systems Security Conference*. NISSC.

[16] 2001. Systems Engineering Fundamentals. (Fort Belvoir, Virginia, 2001).

Discovering Workplace Motivators for the Millennial Generation of IT Employees

Thomas E. Bunton
Purdue University
1016 W. Stadium Ave
West Lafayette, IN 47906
765-496-8282

tb@purdue.edu

Jeffrey L. Brewer
Purdue University
401 N. Grant St
West Lafayette, IN 47907
765-496-6838

jbrewer@purdue.edu

ABSTRACT
This paper provides an overview on motivational research and describes the research methodology and approach that was used to identify the workplace rewards and motivators that the youngest generation of employees, the millennial generation or generation Y, finds attractive in organizations looking to hire them for fulltime Information Technology (IT) positions. Preliminary findings from a pilot study conducted at Purdue University are shared.

Categories and Subject Descriptors
K.7.1 [**Computing Milieux**]: The Computing Profession – *Occupations.*

General Terms
Management, Measurement, Design, Economics, Experimentation, Human Factors.

Keywords
Information Technology, Human Resources, Millennial, Generation Y, Motivators, Rewards

1. INTRODUCTION
Previous generations of employees entered the workforce with the expectations of having one employer their entire career, yearly predicable raises, promotions through seniority, and retiring with a pension and lifelong healthcare. Times have changed and these motivators are no longer financially or organizationally feasible. Additionally, what motivated the previous generations of employees to work hard or at one particular employer over another may not be considered important to the millennial generation. Organizations looking to attract and retain this new generation of employees will need to take a close look at their total benefits package including pay, benefits, learning and development opportunities, and the work environment.

This research aimed to develop and test a methodology that could be used to identify the motivating factors that the millennial generation prefers when seeking full-time employment in IT. The

millennial generation is the group of individuals born on or after 1980 and first entered the workforce in 2004 (Hershatter & Epstien, 2010). According to Trunk (2007), there are "76 million members of Generation Y" (p.1). As of 2010, 35 million millennials were employed in the United State of America and by 2014 this number is projected to be at 58 million (Sujansky & Ferri-Reed, 2010). Organizations can benefit from this research by using it as a stepping-stone to further explore how they can begin to shift their company's approach to rewarding the newest generation of employees.

The research methodology was based off of work originally developed by researchers This and Lippitt which included a Workplace Motivation Checklist containing 25 motivational attributes. Dated motivators were removed and current motivational attributes were added. The methodology expanded on this previous research by adding four rank order type questions and four dichotomous questions within a total rewards framework.

Following the development of the research methodology, a pilot study was conducted at Purdue University by means of a web-based survey. The study was distributed to students currently working part time as IT employees for Purdue University departments or enrolled as juniors or seniors majoring in Purdue University's College of Technology Computer Information Technology or Computer Graphics Technology departments. The study was also distributed through email, discussion boards, and Facebook groups to full-time IT professionals working throughout the state of Indiana via various professional networks such as the Association of Information Technology Professionals East Central Indiana Chapter (AITPECI), DeveloperTown, StartupDigest, Indy Java Users Group, and VergeIndy. The survey restricted participation to only individuals that would be classified as the millennial generation (individuals born between 1980 and 2000) and to those individuals who have full-time IT careers or intend to pursue full-time IT employment in the future.

2. EXISTING RESEARCH
2.1 Workplace Rewards and Motivators
What motivates generations has been an ongoing discussion for decades. One can recognize that each generation is perceived differently by looking at the various generational stereotypes that exist today. Matures or traditionalists are those individuals born between 1922 and 1945 and are said to value conformity and sacrifice, but are risk adverse and resistant to change (Clare, 2009). Boomers or Baby Boomers were born between 1946 and 1963 and are believed to be optimistic and value personal growth, but are idealists (Clare, 2009). Generation X, or Xers, are born

between 1964 and early 1980s. They are said to be techno-literate, but are independent and value their needs before their employers (Clare, 2009).

Millennials, the last generation to enter the workforce, were born between the early 1980s and 2000 (Clare, 2009). They are thought to be sociable, street smart, and eager to learn, but expect rewards for just showing up and lack loyalty (Clare, 2009). Millennials are "accustomed to receiving a great deal of praise from parents and teachers and some have a hard time accepting seemingly negative feedback" (Sujansky & Ferri-Reed, 2010, p. 14).

Although anecdotal information tends to dominate the popular press, there has been some empirical research conducted that help to identify what motivates the different generations of employees in the workforce. Additionally, some research has been replicated since the 1960s that provides valuable insight into possible motivational differences between generations.

Finally, much of the research identified focuses on college or university graduates and what motivators they identify as important. Very little research identifies specific motivators for a particular career type. A review of two studies that examine motivators for high-tech employees will help to identify if particular motivators should be used for recruiting and retaining university graduates pursuing full-time Information Technology (IT) employment.

2.2 Motivational Variations Between Generations

In order to understand how motivational factors have changed over the decades and across different generations of employees, one must examine how motivational factors vary across generations. In one study, researchers Jurkiewicz and Brown (1998) indicated they didn't believe generational cohorts were valid predictors of motivation. In the overall Chi-Square analysis, only four of the 15 attributes exhibited significance in their analysis (Jurkiewicz & Brown, 1998). They believe that "It appears likely that life stages more so than generational cohort explain employee motivation at work." (Jurkiewicz & Brown, 1998, p. 29)

In another research study examining the motivational factors, among other things, of Boomers and GenX, Smola and Sutton (2002) indicate their "results suggest that generational work values do differ" (p. 363). Smola and Sutton (2002) found that "Analysis of the 20 items of this study support these assessments and statistical analysis suggests that Gen X-ers work values are significantly different from those of Baby Boomers." (Smola & Sutton, 2002, p. 378)

James Westerman and Jeanne Yamamura conducted a similar study of generational differences in work environment fit and their ability to retain staff between Boomers and Generation X (Westerman & Yamamura, 2007). In their study, the combined Generation X and Y into a single cohort for purposes of further analysis and hypothesis testing as their t-tests confirmed the lack of significant differences between the two generations (Westerman & Yamamura, 2007). The "primary finding of this study is that work environment fit (specifically goal orientation and system fit) is significantly predictive of employee outcomes for younger generation employees" (Westerman & Yamamura, 2007, p. 156). For Generation X and Y, goal orientation is a primary factor in employee job satisfaction and their intention to remain, but not for Boomers (Westerman & Yamamura, 2007).

Although Westerman and Yamamura argue that they perceive that Generation Y is no different than Generation X, there are researchers that have focused research strictly on the Generation Y or the millennial generation.

A study by Eddy Ng, Linda Schweitzer, and Sean Lyons of 23,413 millennial undergraduate students from across Canada further explored the motivational factors of the millennial generation (Ng, Schweitzer, & Lyons, 2010). Their study focused on career expectations, advancement expectations, pay expectations, and of importance for this review, work attributes. Work attributes included 16 items such as job security, good people to report to, work-life balance, challenging work, etc. (Ng, et al., 2010). Their research showed that "Millennials rated opportunities for advancement as the most desirable work-related attribute" (Ng, et al., 2010, p. 286). This was followed by good people to work with, good people to report to, good training opportunities/developing new skills, and work-life balance (Ng, et al., 2010). Good starting salary was rated at number nine (Ng, et al., 2010).

In a 2011 report, Ian Barford and Patrick Hester discuss the results from a small survey of 18 government employees, six each from Generation Y, X, and Baby Boomers (Barford & Hester, 2011). They discovered that of the five tests that were statistically significant, one involved statistically significant differences between Generation Y and Generation X and between Generation Y and Baby Boomers (Barford & Hester, 2011). Two involved significant differences between Generation Y and Baby Boomers only, and one between Generation Y and Generation X only (Barford & Hester, 2011). These results indicate that there are motivational differences that exist between generations and that Generation X and Generation Y are not motivated by the same factors.

Another study conducted by the Hidden Brain Drain Task Force involved two large-scale nationally representative surveys. This research identified that similarities existed between the Boomer generation and Generation Y (Hewlett, Sherbin, & Sumberg, 2009).

However, refuting the idea that there are motivational differences between Generation X and Generation Y is a study conducted by Patrick Montana and Janet Lenaghan published in a 1999 report. Montana's and Lenaghan's research was based off a 1960s and 1970s Leslie This and Gordon Lippitt study of 6,000 managers and 500 representatives of different companies and government agencies that were asked to rank six of 25 motivational factors that allowed them to do their best work (Montana & Lenaghan, 1999). They discovered that both Generation X (recent graduates) and Generation Y (current undergraduates) identified the exact same six motivational factors; steady employment, respect for me as a person, good pay, chance for promotion, opportunity for self development and improvement, and large amount of freedom on the job (Montana & Lenaghan, 1999).

They compared these results to the 1960s and 1970s results. The 1970s results provided a close match, however steady employment and chance for promotion were replaced with "opportunities to do interesting work" and "feeling my job was important" (Montana & Lenaghan, 1999, p. 28). Interestingly, the 1960's results overlapped with the 1970s and 1999 study with four of the six categories, "respect for me as a person", "good pay", "opportunity for self-development and improvement", and "large amount of freedom on the job" (Montana & Lenaghan, 1999, p. 28). The results from Montana's and Lenaghan's research indicate that Generation X and Generation Y value similar motivational factors and provide additional support that there are little differences between the two generations.

In 2007 Patrick Montana expanded on his previous research at Hofstra University. Along with Francis Petit, they discovered that Generation X and Generation Y did not share the exact same motivational factors (Montana & Petit, 2008). Their research showed that Generation Y ranked the following six factors as their principal motivators, "respect for me as a person", "good pay", "getting along well with others on the job", "chance for promotion", "opportunity to do interesting work", and "opportunity for self-development and improvement" (Montana & Petit, 2008). "Although the rankings by Generation X and Y were markedly different from earlier generations, they were close to each other", only varying in Generation X preferring "feeling my job is important" over "getting along well with others on the job" (Montana & Petit, 2008, p. 37).

The authors specifically point out that Generation Y ranked "getting along well with others on the job" as the leading motivator of this generation even though it wasn't even chosen in the top six by Generation X (Montana & Petit, 2008). Additionally, Montana and Petit reference another study by This and Lippitt conducted in the 1970s (pre-boomers) and 1980s (boomers) where they report that both of these generations ranked six factors of motivation identical to each other (Montana & Petit, 2008).

2.3 Motivational Variations Between Careers

Much debate occurs with respect to whether various generations are motivated by different motivational factors or attributes. However, to completely understand the research surrounding what motivates millennials entering an IT career, an exploration of literature surrounding motivational preferences of IT employees is needed.

Susan O'Neal (1998) indicates that a total rewards strategy provides an interdisciplinary solution to the complicated problem of recruiting and retaining employees (O'Neal, 1998). A total rewards framework is the process by which everything an employee would receive from an employment relationship is identified and assigned to one of four categories. These four categories are laid out in a two by two quadrant. "The upper two quadrants – pay and benefits – represent transactional rewards" (O'Neal, 1998, p. 8). The lower two quadrants represent the relational rewards of learning and development and the work environment (O'Neal, 1998). O'Neal (1998) states, "These ["gold-collar", Information Technology (IT) workers with "hot skills,"] workers are far more focused on technology and their work environment than on pay and benefits." (p. 10)

Researcher Laura Bottorff corroborates on these findings. Bottorff (2011) states, "Transactional attributes were not found to be more important than relational attributes to surveyed student Millennials – in fact, just the opposite was supported." (p. 27)

James Kochanski and Gerald Ledford in their 2001 article explored the top 15 predictors of retention for technology and scientific professionals. They identify these professionals as "knowledge workers whose work is governed primarily by their own knowledge and expertise rather than by a routine or system" (Kochanski & Ledford, 2001, p. 31). They conducted a study based on the employee value proposition co-sponsored by Nextra, Sibson Consulting Group and WorldatWork (formerly the American Compensation Association) on the attitudes of 210 full-time high-tech employees in the private-sector workforce (Kochanski & Ledford, 2001). "Fully three-quarters of scientific

and technical employees reported that work content was very important or extremely important in determining whether they remained with their current employer" (Kochanski & Ledford, 2001). Additionally, this motivation group was the most highly rated (Kochanski & Ledford, 2001). The other four types of rewards: direct financial, indirect financial, career rewards, and affiliation were rated at 62 to 65% as highly important in their decision (Kochanski & Ledford, 2001).

Researchers Reiner Leschinsky and Judd Michael modified the existing This and Lipitt survey methodology and rather than use a broad population of generational cohorts such as recent college graduates or undergraduates, they used generational cohorts within a specific industry, in this case blue-collar production employees in the wood products industry. "The results of the mean-score ratings show that the motivators good pay and having steady employment are ranked in the top three through all the age groups" (Leschinsky & Michael, 2004, p. 38). Leschinsky and Michael (2004) point out that when compared to the 1999 Montana and Lenaghan studies, "respect for me as a person by my supervisor as the most important motivator followed by good pay and opportunity to do interesting work" were the most important factors (p. 38).

Steven Rumpel and John Medcof conducted similar research but rather than use Employee Value Proposition (EVP) they explored high-tech companies that used a total rewards approach to motivating employees (Rumpel & Medcof, 2006). They indicated "technical workers have an unusual rewards preference profile" (Rumpel & Medcof, 2006, 29). They cited a study conducted by Towers Perrin in which 100% of non-technical respondents indicated pay elements as rewarding (Rumpel & Medcof, 2006). Additionally, Rumpel and Medcof cite three more studies about high-tech companies where pay was not the number one motivating factor, but work environment, learning and development were (Rumpel & Medcof, 2006).

Rumpel and Medcof (2006) state "First, clear evidence is available that [Research and Development] R&D workers value all four reward quadrants, not just the traditional monetary compensation and benefits packages that many firms offer" (p. 32). They continue, "Secondly, it is clear that rewards aligned under the work environment quadrant are the most highly valued by these workers" (Rumpel & Medcof, 2006, p. 32).

2.4 Historical Summary

There is conflicting research about whether motivational preferences can be accurately predicted by an individual's generational cohort. Research is nearly split on whether an employees generational cohort is an accurate predictor of motivational preferences.

Research unveils more consistent results when looking at motivational differences among specific types of employees or lines of work. There appears to be a consensus in the theory that blue-collar workers are motivated by much different factors than what motivates high-tech, knowledge driven workers. Additionally, there is little disagreement that discovering what motivates individuals and rewarding them on what they find important is the key to successfully recruiting and retaining talent.

3. RESEARCH METHODOLOGY
3.1 Design
The goals of the research methodology were three-fold. The first objective was to understand specific motivational attribute

importance. This was achieved by having participants rate various motivational factors on a Likert type scale. This section of the methodology was based off work originally created by Leslie This and Gordon Lippitt in the 1960s. Their original 25 motivational attributes was modified to remove outdated factors such as "having a local employee paper" and expanded to include more modern and IT specific workplace motivators such as "sabbatical leaves for passion or volunteer work", "working for an eco-conscious and socially-aware organization", "having a flat management hierarchy", and the "option to telecommute".

The second objective of the methodology was to understand the importance of each of the total rewards categories. This was achieved by asking participants to rank order four sets of motivators. Within each question set, a motivator representing each of the four total rewards categories of pay, benefits, learning and development, and work environment was included.

The last goal of the methodology was to understand what motivators participants considered important when forced to choose one over the other. This section of the methodology contained a list of four dichotomous questions. These questions also used the total rewards categories. The first two questions paired motivators representing the total rewards categories of pay versus benefits and the last two questions paired learning and development and work environment.

3.2 Pilot Study

The resultant pilot survey was quantitative in nature and was conducted by a web-based survey distributed to current IT students, IT student employees, and full-time IT employees throughout the state of Indiana. The sample population was limited to individuals of the millennial generation, those individuals born between 1980 and 2000, and to those participants that are currently employed as full-time IT employees or anticipate full-time IT employment in the near future.

In order to increase participation and successful completion of the survey, an incentive was offered to participants. Upon successful completion of the survey, participants could choose to have their contact information entered into a separate raffle drawing for one of two $25 iTunes gift cards.

Approval of the research study was requested and received from the university's Institutional Review Board (IRB). It was estimated that participants could complete the survey in less than 10 minutes.

3.3 Units

The survey presented a list of 40 workplace motivational attributes and each participant was asked to rate each of the attributes on a five point Likert scale from 5 (very important) to 1 (unimportant). Similar to the previous studies, the top six primary motivators were identified by statistical analysis. Additionally, ANOVA and Tukey HSD (Honestly Significant Difference) tests were utilized to determine significant differences between the means. The survey also asked a series of four rank order questions. Each rank order question contained a set of four motivators, one motivator from each of the four total reward categories. These rank order questions forced identification of a single motivational factor and subsequent total rewards. Lastly, a set of four dichotomous type questions was asked. These questions were used to identify the most important motivator of the two presented.

3.4 Sample

While the population of the study was the millennial generation of individuals having full-time IT employment or aspirations of pursuing full-time IT employment, the sample population was students currently enrolled in IT courses or as IT employees at Purdue University and individuals employed as full-time IT employees throughout the state of Indiana. The survey methodology restricted participation to those individuals who are members of the millennial generation and who currently have full-time IT employment or anticipate pursuing full-time IT employment in the near future.

3.5 Data Collection

Data collection was performed via the university's Qualtrics survey system. Individuals were provided the solicitation email that included a link to the survey. The survey tool provided two qualifying questions, year of birth and a yes or no question asking whether or not the individual was currently employed as full-time employee or of if they anticipated pursuing full-time IT employment in the future. Individuals that that did not fit the research demographics of birth year ranges outside the research range of 1980 to 2000 or who answered no to the IT career question were directed to the end of the survey and presented with a statement that thanked them for starting the survey, but that they did not qualify to participate in the study.

Qualtrics was set up so that each question block required participants to respond to every question. Additionally, the Qualtrics option to prevent ballot stuffing was enabled to restrict users from taking the survey multiple times. This option prevented those individuals that have already completed the survey from retaking it and also prevented individuals that did not pass the two initial qualifying questions to resubmit their answers.

3.6 Survey Instrument

The survey instrument was divided into 7 blocks or web pages. The first block provided the high-level overview of the study, outlined that it was completely voluntary, that individuals could stop at anytime, and individuals that successfully completed the study would be entitled to enter their email address into a raffle.

The second block provided the two qualifying required questions. Year of birth was the first question and it was collected as four digits. The second question was a yes or no radio button asking the users to indicate whether they were currently working as a full-time IT employee or if they saw themselves pursuing full-time IT employment in the future.

Upon successfully qualifying for the survey, users were provided block three. This block of questions collected the demographic data for research. Demographics collected included gender, graduation status, employment status, and internship status.

Block four and five each provided a list of 20 motivators and individuals were required to rate each one on a Likert type scale, very important to unimportant. Responses of very important were recorded a 5, important as a 4, moderately important as a 3, of little importance as a 2, and unimportant as a 1.

Block six provided participants with a set of four rank order type questions with each question containing a set of four motivators, one motivator from each of the four total rewards categories. The specific motivators and the grouping of what motivators were assigned to each question set was the output from a three step process. The first step was assigning all 40 of the motivators to a total rewards category. The second step was the identification of four motivators from each of the four total rewards categories. The final step was placing each motivator, representing the total rewards category, into the assigned question block. This was completed by grouping one motivator from each of the total rewards categories into a question block consisting of all four total rewards categories. The motivator assignment to a particular question block was determined by the order they appeared in the final list of 40 motivators. Additionally, this set of four questions staggered the presentation of motivators based on total rewards category.

Responses from this set of four questions were recorded in Qualtrics with a rank assigned to each individual motivator item. The highest ranked item was identified with a number one, the second highest with a two, the third highest with a three, and the least important motivator as a four. The score for each motivator item would be transformed within SAS to better match the previous Likert scale used in question block four and five.

Block seven of the survey provided users a set of four dichotomous questions. These questions were developed from the final list of 40 motivators and paired according to researcher interests and committee input. The first two questions in this block paired the total rewards categories of pay versus benefits. The last two questions paired the total rewards categories of learning and development with work environment. Responses for each pair of questions were recorded as a one or a two. A response of one represents the first item in the pairing and a two represents the second item.

Once participants successfully completed the final question block, they were directed to the end of survey message that thanked them for their participation and provided them with the option to be enter the drawing via a separate survey link. This survey link was also set up to prevent ballot stuffing and required participants to be referred to the survey link from the previous research survey.

3.7 Data Manipulation
Data was exported from Qualtrics into a file that contained comma-separated values. The Qualtrics export was cleansed to remove partially completed and non-qualifying responses. Additionally columns not needed for the research such as start and end times, year of birth, etc. were removed as well.

Data was imported into SAS 9.2 for analysis. Direct results from Qualtrics were used in all cases except for question block six, which contained the rank order questions. This set of four questions, each containing four rank order items, were exported from Qualtrics as 16 items. Item one represented the first motivator listed in question one, item two as motivator two, item three as motivator three, item four as motivator four, item five as motivator one in question set two, item six as motivator two in question set two, etc. Rankings of 1 to 4 were assigned to the individual motivators within each question set. 1 indicated the most important item, 2 the second most, 3 to the third most, and 4 to the least important motivator. In order to more closely align with Likert type scale used for the 40 motivators listed in question block four and five, where the very important response was indicated as a 5, the responses for this question block were transformed in SAS so that the most important motivator was assigned a 4, the second most a 3, the third most a 2, and the least important motivator a 1.

4. RESULTS
4.1 Demographics
259 responses were received from an estimated 4,130 possible participants or a response rate of 6.27%. 121 of those participants met the eligibility requirements of birth years, intent to pursue or currently having IT careers, and completed the survey. 100 individuals submitted their email address in the additional survey to be entered into the drawing for two $25 iTunes gift cards. 102 individuals were male and 19 were female. 109 of the participants were still students and 12 had graduated. 28 participants were unemployed, 69 were employed part-time, and 24 indicated they were employed full-time. 61 participants indicated they had an IT internship as a student and 60 indicated they had no internship.

4.2 Preliminary Findings
When examining the results of the pilot study conducted at Purdue University that was based off of historical research aimed at identifying the top motivators simply by mean response alone, the motivator "respect for me as a person" was rated as most important. However, statistical tests showed that there were no significant differences between the top seven motivators. The only motivator to make the top seven that wasn't in the original study that researchers This and Lippitt conducted was "good health insurance coverage". Surprisingly, unlike previous studies, the motivator of "good pay" didn't make the list of top motivators.

However, it is interesting to note that when presented with the choice of either having "increased pay" or "longer vacation allowances", participants choose increased pay. Additionally, when participants were required to select between "increased stock options" or "reduced health insurance costs", participants chose "reduced health insurance costs".

A total rewards methodology was applied to the rank order type questions and the 40 motivators. In the rank order type questions, where there was an equal number of motivators representing all the total rewards categories, the motivators representing the total rewards category of pay were highest ranked. Similarly, when reviewing the 40 motivators within their specific total rewards grouping, pay was statistically different than learning and development.

Additionally, when the rank order type questions and 40 motivators were categorized into their total rewards groupings of transactional or relational based rewards, participants showed a statistical preference for motivators that represented the total rewards group of transactional rewards over relational.

The methodology also aimed to determine whether or not demographic factors such as gender, employment status, and history of an IT internship was related to the importance ratings millennials assigned to workplace motivators.

When reviewing gender across all 40 motivators, male and female participants only had statistically significant different ratings for two of the 40 motivators. When looking at the four dichotomous questions, male and female participants only had one question that resulted in statistically significant differences, males preferred "pay" over "longer vacation allowances" and females preferred the opposite.

When reviewing the motivators within the total rewards framework, there was no statistical difference between male and female participants in the four sets of rank order type questions. When reviewing the 40 individual motivators assigned in a total rewards categories, male and female participants had statistically significant differences in the ratings they assigned to learning and development. Females preferred it more than men.

Lastly, when reviewing the total rewards groupings of transactional and relational based rewards, neither the rank order type question nor the 40 motivators assigned to their total rewards grouping resulted in any statistically significant differences between male and female participants.

The study also aimed at understanding if participants' employment status could be a factor in motivational preference. In five of the 40 motivators, the participants' employment status resulted in statistically significant differences in motivational ratings. Unemployed individuals rated "good pensions" as more important than those employed part-time. Participants employed full-time rated the motivators "large amounts of freedom on the job", "culture of high performing staff", and "access to social media at work", as more important than the other employment classes. Participants employed full-time also rated the workplace motivator of "company discounts and purchasing programs" less important than those employed part-time. Employment status had no statistical significant impact on the four dichotomous questions.

Lastly, the study aimed at trying to understand if internship was a factor in workplace motivational rating. In six of the 40 motivators, the participants' internship status resulted in statistically different motivator ratings. Individuals that did not have an internship rated "constant feedback" less important over those that did have an IT internship, but they rated "fair vacation arrangements", "large amounts of freedom", "flexible work and telecommuting", "relaxed dress policy" and "good health insurance coverage" as more important than participants that did have an internship. Finally, those individuals that had no internship preferred a "culture of high performing staff" over a "defined mentoring relationship", whereas those that did have an IT internship slightly preferred "defined mentoring relationships" over a "culture of high performing staff".

5. CONCLUSIONS

This research was aimed at developing a methodology to identify the top workplace motivators and attributes that the millennial generation prefers when having or seeking full time IT employment. It combined two broad categories of research, specifically generational studies of motivation and career path or job type motivational preferences. In order to enhance the study's reliability, the framework was composed of three methods to measure motivator preferences, starting with a Likert type scale, to a set of rank order type questions, and lastly by requiring participants to select one motivator over another.

6. REFERENCES

[1] Barford, I. N., & Hester, P. T. (2011). *Analysis of generation y workforce motivation using multiattribute utility theory.* Retrieved from Defense Acquisition University website: http://www.dau.mil/pubscats/ARJ_Library/ARJ57/Barford_ARJ57.pdf

[2] Bottorff, L. M. (2011). Work attribute importance and loyalty intention: Millennial generation psychological contract. CMC Senior Theses. Retrieved from http://scholarship.claremont.edu/cmc_theses/110/

[3] Clare, C. (2009). Generational differences: Turning challenges into opportunities. *Journal of Property Management, 74*(5), 40-43.

[4] Hershatter, A., & Epstein, M. (2010) Millennials and the world of work: An organization and management perspective. *Journal of Business and Psychology, 25*,2, 211-223.

[5] Hewlett, S. A., Sherbin, L., & Sumberg, K. (2009). How gen y & boomers will reshape your agenda. *Harvard Business Review, 87*(7/8), 71-76.

[6] Jurkiewicz, C. E. , & Brown, R. G. (1998). GenXers vs boomers vs matures: generational comparisons of public employee motivation. *Review of Public Personnel Administration, 18,* 18-37.

[7] Kochanski, J., & Ledford, G. (2001). "How to keep me" – Retaining technical professionals. *Research Technology Management, 44*(3), 31-38.

[8] Leschinsky, R. M., & Michael, J. H. (2004). Motivators and desired company values of wood products industry employees: Investigating generational differences. *Forest Products Journal, 54*(1), 34-39.

[9] Montana, P. J., & Lenaghan, J. A. (1999). What motivates and matters most to generations x and y. *NACE Journal, 59*(4), 27-30.

[10] Montana, P. J., & Petit, F. (2008). Motivating and managing generation x and y on the job while preparing for z: A market oriented approach. *Journal of Business & Economics Research, 6*(8), 35-39.

[11] Ng, E. S., Schweitzer, L., & Lyons, S. T. (2010). New generation, great expectations: A field study of the millennial generation. *Journal of Business & Psychology, 25*(2), 281-292.

[12] O'Neal, S. (1998). The phenomenon of total rewards. *ACA Journal, Autumn,* 6-18.

[13] Rumpel, S., & Medcof, J. W. (2006). Total rewards: Good fit for tech workers. *Research Technology Management, 49*(5), 27-35.

[14] Smola, K. W., & Sutton, C. D. (2002). Generational differences: revisiting generational work values for the new millennium. *Journal of Organizational Behavior, 23,* 363-382. doi:10.1002/job.147

[15] Sujansky, J. G., & Ferri-Reed, J. (2010). Motivate your millennial employees. *Supervision, 71*(4), 13-15.

[16] Trunk, P. (2007). What gen y really wants. *Time.* Retrieved September 18, 2011 from http://www.time.com/time/magazine/article/0,9171,1640395,00.html.

[17] Westerman, J. W., & Yamamura, J. H. (2007). Generational preferences for work environment fit: effects on employee outcomes. *Career Development International, 12*(2), 150-161. doi:10.1108/1362043071073

Identifying and Evaluating Information Technology Bachelor's Degree Programs

Barry M. Lunt
Brigham Young University
Information Technology
Provo, Utah
luntb@byu.edu

Bikalpa Neupane
Brigham Young University
Information Technology
Provo, Utah
bikalpa_neupane@byu.net

Andrew Hansen
Brigham Young University
Information Technology
Provo, Utah
andrewhansen@byu.edu

Richard Ofori
Brigham Young University
Information Technology
Provo, Utah nanaofori76@yahoo.co.uk

ABSTRACT

This paper describes the process for identifying and evaluating Information Technology (IT) bachelor's programs in the United States, in an effort to answer the question, how many IT bachelor's programs are there in the US? Due to widespread variation in the names of academic degree programs, one cannot simply count those named Information Technology. At SIGITE 2011, a framework was presented for identifying IT programs and for evaluating their compliance to an accepted standard. This framework, with slight modifications, has been applied throughout this research. We first compiled a list of prospective IT programs to research. Each university on the list was researched by looking at their university webpage in search of a list of computing majors listed at that university. If, at a glance, these program's required courses look similar to those required in an IT program, the program was evaluated and given a numerical score compliance factor, as compared to the standard, no matter the name of the major. This compliance factor is calculated using the assessment form that is included in this document. The results of this analysis are presented.

Categories and Subject Descriptors

K.2.3 [Information systems education]

General Terms

Computing Programs, Information Technology

Keywords

Information Technology; Model Curriculum

1. INTRODUCTION

What is an Information Technology program? How do we identify Information Technology programs amongst other computing programs? And, once an IT program is found, how well does it conform to an accepted standard?

The Special Interest Group for Information Technology Education (SIGITE) of the Association for Computing Machinery (ACM) set out to answer these questions. SIGITE was interested in determining how many IT programs exist nationwide. As of this writing, there are 18 IT programs accredited by CAC of ABET in the USA.

The results of this research will enable further studies of IT programs in the US, including job placement, GPA, graduate studies, etc.

2. METHODS

2.1 Identification of Potential IT Programs

Because not all IT programs are named "Information Technology," a list of potential IT programs needed to be created. This list needed to include all potential IT programs, ideally. Each potential IT program needed to be compared to the IT Model Curriculum [1]. To create this list, each of the three researchers was given the task of searching for their own list of IT programs. These lists were to be obtained with the following criteria:

- The list should contain all of the 18 ABET-accredited IT programs.
- The list should have a large number of programs in common with the other researcher's lists.
- The list should be as comprehensive as possible without becoming too large.

Using the Internet, we then searched for sources for these lists. Once each researcher was confident that their list met the above criteria, a comparison was made between all of the lists. This comparison looked for overlap and inclusion of all the ABET-accredited IT programs. These individual lists were later combined. This combination process will be discussed later. The combined list will be referenced as the "master list" for convenience.

Perhaps the most helpful resource was the National Center for Education Statistics College Navigator. [3] The master list relied heavily on this source due to its comprehensive data and ease of use. This resource was able to query a National Education Statistics database to include the names of majors that could potentially be IT programs. After a combination of the three initial lists was made, we found that some of the ABET-accredited IT programs were not included. This issue led to a need for broader search criteria in this resource to include these IT programs. In the end, the entire category of "Computer and Information Sciences and Support Services," was required to include all the ABET-accredited IT programs and other potential programs under the same definition (See Figure 1).

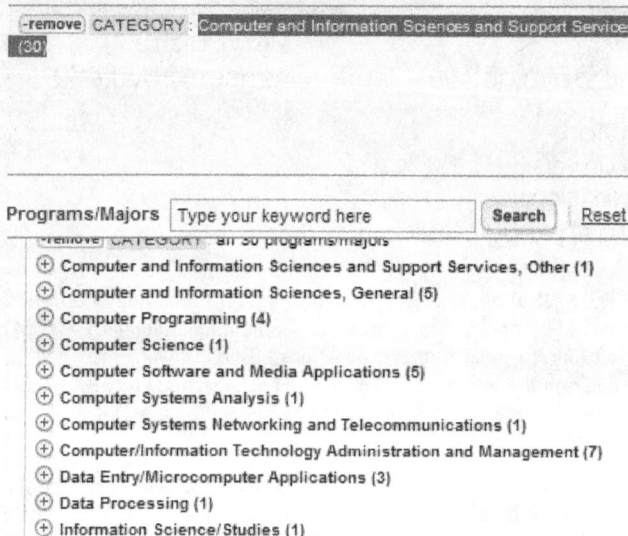

-remove CATEGORY : Computer and Information Sciences and Support Services (30)

Programs/Majors Type your keyword here   Search   Reset

-remove CATEGORY: all 30 programs/majors
⊕ Computer and Information Sciences and Support Services, Other (1)
⊕ Computer and Information Sciences, General (5)
⊕ Computer Programming (4)
⊕ Computer Science (1)
⊕ Computer Software and Media Applications (5)
⊕ Computer Systems Analysis (1)
⊕ Computer Systems Networking and Telecommunications (1)
⊕ Computer/Information Technology Administration and Management (7)
⊕ Data Entry/Microcomputer Applications (3)
⊕ Data Processing (1)
⊕ Information Science/Studies (1)

Figure 1 Screenshot of Majors included in the NCES filtered search

This was primarily because the University of Florida has an ABET-accredited IT program named "Computing and Information Sciences, Information Technology, BS." This meant that the University of Florida would only be included in the list if the entire category was included. Drexel also has its IT major in the "College of Information Sciences and Technology". Other ABET-accredited IT programs were named "Computer and Information Technology" (Purdue University at West Lafayette) and "Computing with concentration in Information Technology" (Indiana University-Purdue University Indianapolis).

Once a complete list from the National Center for Education Statistics College Navigator was obtained, the creation of the master list took place. Each researcher's list was combined with the College Navigator List. The three lists were of different size and came from different sources. Overlap was calculated by removing duplicates from the combined list in a Microsoft Excel spreadsheet. The compiled list of all three individual lists contained 909 academic institutions, with 291 duplicates between all three lists, and included all 18 ABET-accredited IT programs.

This extensive list compilation and combination process was taken to ensure that no potential IT program was excluded, that all ABET-accredited IT programs were included, and to ensure a comprehensive research project without evaluating all the >2000 institutions of higher education in the US.

2.1 Removing Evaluation Bias

Once this master list was compiled, there was a need to remove bias in evaluations of the identified programs. To do this, three ABET-accredited IT programs were chosen for all three researchers to evaluate independently within a week. Then, the three results were compared with all the researchers and each

researcher had to explain why they scored each topic the way they did. If disagreements arose, further investigation into the course catalogue and class descriptions by all the researchers was taken until a unanimous score was reasoned. This process was overseen by the lead researcher, an IT professor and member of SIGITE. Any major topic that was not within 2 points of the other researchers was investigated further in the manner described. This process was repeated for a total of 7 ABET-accredited IT programs. The results were then compiled.

2.2 Identifying an IT Curriculum

Many of the programs on the master list would not be considered IT programs. To determine if each program was a potential IT program, each institution on the list went through a web research process, which entailed the following procedures:

1. Visiting the Official University Webpage.

2. Finding a list of all computing majors or a comprehensive list of majors for that university.

3. Determining if each computing major looks like IT:

   a) Must contain most of the 5 "pillars of IT" (See Figure 2).

Programs with questionable identities were consulted upon with other researchers and the lead researcher. Once a program was identified to be a potential IT program, an evaluation of the compliance factor took place.

2.3 Evaluating the programs

Programs were evaluated using the following procedures:

1) Visit the official webpage of the identified university.

2) If possible, obtain a current university course catalog.

3) If possible, obtain a required courses listing for the major to be evaluated.

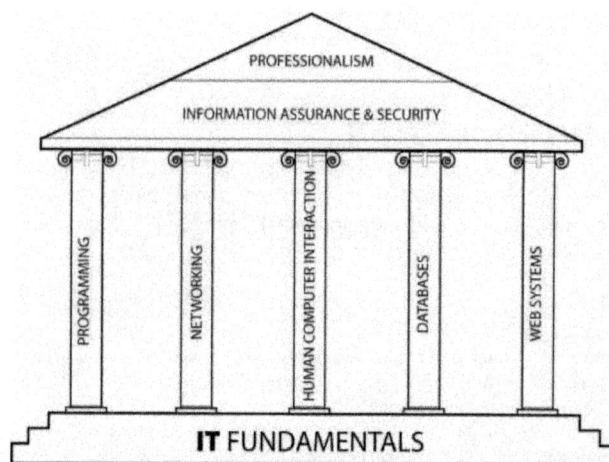

Figure 2 - Pillars of Information Technology [1]

4) Using both the course catalog and course listings/ descriptions, evaluate the compliance using the assessment framework. [2] This is described further below.

5) Compute IT Compliance Factor from the assessment framework.

These programs were evaluated using the 2008 SIGITE Model Curriculum [1] for four-year bachelors programs, and the assessment framework for identifying IT programs from proceedings of the 2011 SIGITE conference. [2] In summary, evaluation of a program's curriculum involved using a table and reference curriculum as a checklist. The evaluation process is described as follows from the assessment framework: "Measures are assessed using a simple point system. If a measure is met by the institution's curriculum, a point is awarded. If a measure is not met, no point is given. This simple scoring system will allow programs that exceed a stated threshold to be classified as fully conforming programs; it will also provide a simple indicator to the portion of IT 2008 compliant content for partially conforming programs. Each point corresponds to the IT Body of Knowledge summary found on page 27 of the 2008 Model Curriculum." [2] [6] An ideal form (Table 1) and a sample evaluation (Table 2) are given below.

The data from each of these forms were compiled and sorted. This research shows that all 909 institutions fall into the following categories in the spreadsheet:

- Identified as IT and evaluated (given a compliance factor score).
- Identified as not IT (no compliance factor score).
- Identified as IT initially but the evaluation was stopped before completion due to low compliance.

Table 1 – Assessment Summary (Performed against Website)

IT 2008 Body of Knowledge Core Topic Title	Module Type		Points Available
	Core	Elective	
IT Fundamentals	4		4
Human Computer Interaction	7		7
Information Assurance and Security	11		11
Information Management	6		6
Integrative Programming & Techniques	7		7
Mathematics and Statistics for IT	7		7
Foundations of Networking	6		6
Programming Fundamentals	5		5
Platform Technologies	6		6
System Administration and Maintenance	4		4
System Integration and Architecture	7		7
Social and Professional Issues	9		9
Web Systems and Technologies	6		6
TOTAL	85	0	85
Weighted Total (multiply TOTAL by 2)	1.000	0.000	1.00
Instructions for Weighted Total Calculation	Divide total by 85 and enter above	Divide total by 170 and enter above	
Core Coverage (Sum of weighted totals *2)	2.000		2.00
Capstone Experience (0.5 pts/semester)	1		1.00
Core content less than 50% of total content?	1		1.00
Final Compliance Factor (total of 3 values)	*4.000*		4.00

2.4 Reasons for Not Evaluating a Program

Most decisions made on evaluation were made in the identification process, including the decision to not evaluate at all, or to evaluate despite a seemingly low compliance. Some decisions to discontinue evaluation occurred mid-evaluation. The primary reasons for not evaluating a listed program are as follows:

- Program focus on algorithms, AI, or graphics (looked like Computer Science (CS))

Table 2 – BYU IT Program Evaluation

IT 2008 Body of Knowledge Core Topic Title	Module Type		Points Available
	Core	Elective	
IT Fundamentals	4		4
Human Computer Interaction	7		7
Information Assurance and Security	9		11
Information Management	6		6
Integrative Programming & Techniques	5		7
Mathematics and Statistics for IT	6		7
Foundations of Networking	6		6
Programming Fundamentals	4		5
Platform Technologies	2		6
System Administration and Maintenance	2		4
System Integration and Architecture	3		7
Social and Professional Issues	7		9
Web Systems and Technologies	6		6
TOTAL	67	0	85
Weighted Total (multiply TOTAL by 2)	0.788	0.000	1.00
Instructions for Weighted Total Calculation	Divide total by 85 and enter above	Divide total by 170 and enter above	
Core Coverage (Sum of weighted totals *2)	1.576		2.00
Capstone Experience (0.5 pts/semester)	1		1.00
Core content less than 50% of total content?(award 1 if yes, 0 if no)	1		1.00
Final Compliance Factor (total of 3 values)	*3.576*		4.00

- Program focus on management, accounting, or e-commerce (looked like Information Systems (ISYS))
- Website in Spanish, mostly the case for Puerto Rico.
- Website did not provide enough information (no course catalogue, list of majors, or course descriptions)

2.5 Modifications of the Evaluation Form

After the initial scoring of ABET-accredited IT programs, some modifications were needed on the assessment form. These included:

- Scoring of the capstone to be one point instead of two points. This was based simply on inclusion of a capstone course/program. The reason for this change was that the largest compliance factor was 4, and 2 was too large a weight. It also allows accommodating programs on a semester or quarter system.
- The Weighted Total to be out of 2 instead of 1. This change was to increase the weight of the other courses included in the evaluation.

3. CURRENT RESULTS

The compiled master list consisted of 909 institutions with computing programs. Of those, approximately 350 went through some of the identification process. Of those 350 programs, 220 were identified as being close enough to IT programs that they were assigned compliance factor scores according to curriculum fit. Some programs lacked sufficient information on the Web to permit an assessment. All 18 ABET accredited IT programs were evaluated and found to have high compliance factors.

Of the programs evaluated, there were a few trends:

- Human Computer Interaction (HCI) was often lacking in programs
- "Applied Computer Science" programs were most likely IT
- Some programs were called IT but did not include the IT pillars, and were actually ISYS, CS, etc.
- Some hybrid majors were included: "Information Systems Technology," "Computer Science Technology", "Computer and Information Science".
- Many technical institutions offered concentrations in specific IT pillars.
- As might be expected, few, if any, "CS" labeled programs were actually IT.

The end product of this research is the comprehensive, sorted list of all evaluated IT programs with their associated compliance factor. This includes the compliance factors of the universities in a summarized form. Table 3 gives an example of this.

Table 3: Universities and Their Associated Compliance Factors

University	Campus	Name of Major	Compliance Factor
Brigham Young University	Provo, UT	Information Technology	3.576
Southern Polytechnic State University	Marietta, GA	Information Technology	3.74
New Jersey Institute of Technology	Newark, NJ	Information Technology	3.859
…	…	…	…

Since the complete table of these findings is much too large to be included in this paper, it can be found at:

http://www.et.byu.edu/~luntb/SIGITE/index.html. This URL includes a table of all the 220 institutions included in the analysis, sorted both by institution name and by their respective compliance factor. It also includes the master list of the 909 institutions with which this research began.

Another very interesting part of our findings are in Table 4, which lists the different names the IT programs were known by, and the respective number of each. Gratifyingly, we see that the majority of these programs that we would consider to be IT programs are titled, Information Technology. But it is indeed interesting to see the range of other names used.

Table 4: Various Names of Evaluated IT Programs

Program Name	# of Occurrences
Information Technology	113
Computer Information Systems	19
IT concentration/emph. in Computer Science	9
Computer IT	6
Information Systems	6
Computer Information Science	4
Computer and IT	3
Computer and Information Science(s)	3
Applied Computer Science	2
Computer Security	2
Computing and IT	2
Information Sciences & Technologies	2
IT concentration in Computer Information Systems	2
IT Management	2
IT and Systems	2
IT Systems	2
Advancing Computer Science	1
Applied Computer Science & Information Systems	1
Applied Computing Systems & Technology	1
Applied IT	1
Computer Information Systems & Security	1
Computer Information Systems & Technology	1
Computer Science & Networking	1
Computer Systems	1
Computer Systems Management Applications	1
Computer Systems Science	1
Computer Technology Management	1
Information and Computer Technology	1
Information and Technology Management	1
Information Assurance & Security	1
Information Assurance/Network & IT Administration	1
Information Engineering Technology	1
Information Management & Technology	1
Information Science	1
Information Science, Systems & Technology	1
Information Security	1
Information Systems Management	1
Information Systems & Technology	1
Information Systems concentration in	1

Computer Science	
IT and Business	1
IT Applications	1
IT concentration in Business Administration	1
IT concentration in Professional Studies	1
IT emphasis in Computing Technology	1
IT Engineering	1
IT Leadership	1
IT option in Information Systems	1
IT and Informatics	1
IT and Management	1
IT and Security	1
IT and Web Science	1
IT-Systems & Security	1
IT track in Computer Science	1
Management Information Systems	1
Network and System Administration	1
Networking emphasis in Computer Science	1
Technology Information Systems	1

We also found that of these 220 programs that were evaluated, 210 (95.5%) of them were BS programs, 7 (3.2%) of them were BA programs, 2 (0.9%) of them were BAS (Bachelors of Applied Science) programs, and 1 (0.5%) was a BAT (Bachelors of Applied Technology) program.

This research has become increasingly more important as new programs and trends are being discovered. This research will be used to reach out to IT educators in the nation, establish a larger IT community, and further define and identify IT as an academic discipline.

4. ACKNOWLEDGMENTS

This research has been sponsored by SIGITE, a special-interest group of the ACM.

5. REFERENCES

[1] LUNT, B. M., EKSTROM, J. J., GORKA, S., HISLOP, G., KAMALI, R., LAWSON, E., LEBLANC, R., MILLER, J. AND REICHGELT, H. Curriculum Guidelines for Undergraduate Degree Programs in Information Technology, ACM, 2008, http://www.acm.org//education/curricula/IT2008%20Curriculum.pdf

[2] ROWE, D. C., LUNT, B. M. AND HELPS, R. G. An assessment framework for identifying information technology programs. In Proceedings of the Proceedings of the 2011 conference on Information technology education (West Point, New York, USA, 2011). ACM, West Point, 2011.

[3] A-Z, S. I. (n.d.). College Navigator - Search Results. National Center for Education Statistics (NCES) Home Page, a part of the U.S. Department of Education. Retrieved February 20, 2012, from http://nces.ed.gov/collegenavigator/?s=all&p=11&l=5&ic=1

Testing & Quantifying ERP Usability

Nancy E. Parks
Department of Information Design & Corporate Communication
Bentley University, 175 Forrest Drive, Waltham, MA, USA
parks_nanc@bentley.edu

ABSTRACT

An Enterprise Resource Planning (ERP) system benefits the business, although the typically complex interface can challenge end users whose errors can undermine the benefits of real-time automation. Many prior studies of ERP users measured attitudes rather than use of the ERP. In contrast, this research involved testing users as they worked with PeopleSoft™ to complete an inventory procedure. An experiment measured success and time while users completed a task using the multi-screen default interface and a simplified single-screen version. Complexity of the interfaces was quantified with two models. GOMS-KLM described the interface in cognitive terms and a visual model described the design. The default complex screens required almost twice as many steps to navigate seven times the number of on-screen elements. Trends and participant comments validated the importance of interface usability, although complexity was a significant variable only for time spent working on the task, not success. Task success was dependent on each user scanning and verifying data before submitting it, an observed behavior. In this paper two studies are presented from a larger effort blending human factors and empirical methods to assess ERP usability and to demonstrate the importance of measuring usability and actual use, not just attitudes about an ERP.

Categories and Subject Descriptors: H.5.2.

Keywords: ERP Usability, ERP Complexity, Applied GOMS-KLM's, ERP User Task Success, ERP Task Time, ERP Screen Customization

1 INTRODUCTION

Enterprise Resource Planning (ERP) systems are sophisticated information databases that automate cross-functional business processes critical for competitive advantage. ERP users, however, often encounter challenges using the typically complex ERP interface. ERP users recognize both the value and usability challenge an ERP system can represent. One participant in this study described the ERP as, "A source of many jokes and derogatory comments about how it impacts daily work." Other participants noted how the ERP is well-regarded as "a vital anchor tool" and "integral" to the business.

Most prior studies of ERP users have relied upon question-based instruments addressing perception about ERP technology as indicators of adoption, without correlating those findings to a user's work with the ERP. A business relies upon success-based measures about ERP use, less so the user's perception of the system. This research effort combined human factors and empirical study methods to explore the question, '*What impact does the complexity of ERP interfaces have on end-user success and task time while completing a transaction?*'

An experiment measured success and time as users completed inventory tasks using the default, complex interface, and a reworked, simpler version. The default Material Transfer interface in PeopleSoft™ was the complex screen. The simple screen was a custom-developed html form based on universal design principles.

Quantifying what makes an ERP interface complex or simple was a supplementary undertaking to describe complexity in meaningful terms. The Galitz [9] visual complexity model and the Kieras [15] GOMS–KLM model were applied to both the screen versions participants used to complete the inventory task. The models provided measures for the complexity of the two interfaces tested in the experiment.

2 LITERATURE REVIEW

A human factors approach involves watching users work with technology to see how well the interface supports task completion and meets expectations [27]. GOMS-KLM's and visual complexity are two models from the human factors field that emerged from these types of user studies working with interfaces used to guide design improvements. Many prior studies of ERP users have focused on user attitudes and perceptions, not their successful completion of required tasks.

2.1 Observing and Modelling Human Interaction with Technology

In 1983, Stuart Card, Thomas Moran, and Allen Newell collaborated to map the cognitive steps humans undertake when interacting with technology. They conducted a series of experiments observing adults completing word processing tasks and produced a task-based model based on the Goals, Operators, and Methods for each step a user takes, along with the Selections made, GOMS. Keystroke Level Measures, KLM's, they introduced as a simpler version that others could use.

Liu et al. [18] applied the GOMS-KLM model to estimate times in driving studies. Wood and Kieras [29] used them for improving the design of a stock web site. GOMS-KLM's have also been used to identify design trade-offs in credit card mail processing systems [19], interactions in cell phone interfaces [10], and improvements in medical health record interfaces [23]. The model does have limitations.

The GOMS-KLM model excludes trial and error loops, which are typical when people work with technology. User expertise is another variable the GOMS-KLM model does not account for because the mental operators and rules apply regardless of a user's skill or prior use of the interface. The Kieras [15] KLM model adjusted time estimates for keying based on typing skill. Finally, the GOMS-KLM model lacks the ability to account for the visual complexity of an interface, although complexity is suggested by more steps and longer task time estimates.

Galitz [9] simplified a Tullis model for calculating visual complexity as part of his synthesis of interface design principles. A composite score for complexity results from counting all objects, all horizontal, and all vertical alignments within the interface, then adding them together. Combined, the GOMS-KLM and Galitz models provide a relevant quantitative measure for interface complexity.

2.2 Prior Studies of ERP Users

Research about ERP users is an under-studied topic in the Information Systems literature [3][12]. ERP user studies undertaken address the adoption or attitudes, perceptions, and user intent to work with ERP technology that could contribute to a more successful ERP implementation or upgrade [8]. Among the ERP user studies reviewed, four distinct perceptual categories emerge : *Satisfaction* [24][30][32]; *Usefulness* [11][7]; *Ease of Use* [28][7]; and, *Acceptance* [4][21][5][3]. Often these user perceptions are inter-related, and training is related to them all. In a business setting, however, ERP adoption is required, not optional [31]. A business expects consistent, successful use of the system, whether it is easy to use or not.

2.3 Reassessing ERP Usability

Studies of ERP usability are rare in the literature [11][26]. This is possibly explained by the fact that ERP systems are not designed to delight the end-user with ease of use. Instead, the business process, not the end-user, drives ERP interface design [1].

Poor interface usability of ERP systems might erode some of the very gains an ERP provides a business in terms of real-time information and process automation. When users work with the ERP interface correctly, they accurately key data, the business realizes production targets, and ships complete, on-time customer orders. Where a difficult-to-use cell phone or spreadsheet interface might frustrate a single user, mistakes made in an ERP can have far-reaching consequences for the business. Mis-keyed amounts flow through the system and affect production quantities so that customer orders may fall short of commitments.

An emphasis on attitudes independent of observations of users working with the ERP in the prior studies may have missed important details that could help improve use of ERP system in the workplace. Might small improvements in easier-to-use ERP interfaces translate to higher profit margins by eliminating waste and rework? This research sought improvement opportunities by studying users as they worked with the ERP and testing how the complexity of the ERP interface affected task performance, specifically success and time spent completing the task.

3 METHODOLOGY

In PeopleSoft™ the Material Transfer task, called a Bin-to-Bin procedure by the business, automates the process of storing or consuming materials used in the production of finished goods. The transaction, performed thousands of times a day, was the basis for this study of PeopleSoft task completion and time on task. The study tested participants as they completed the material transfer task to explore the main research question about ERP interface complexity. Success and task time were the dependent variables in this study because a business requires correct, efficient use of the ERP system and accurate data with every transaction.

3.1 Experiment

The principal designed an experiment to test the effect of ERP interface complexity by having participants complete an inventory transfer task using two different versions of the ERP interface, the default complex interface and a reworked, simple version. Two measures tested the impact of ERP complexity on user performance: task completion success and task time, variables that are important to a business.

The principal conducted forty-two experimental lab sessions over a two-week period. Participants completed the same inventory transfer task two times, using different scenarios and working with two versions of the inventory transfer screen. The simple screen version of the interface was designed to support user success by combining process flow and universal design principles. The default PeopleSoft inventory interface represented the complex screen. Data from four of the lab sessions were excluded, so the final data set included results for 38 participants, 19 who perform the procedure as part of their normal work, and 19 who do not.

3.1.1 Participants

Participants included adults aged 18 and older who use computers daily in their work at a U.S. manufacturing business. Half of the participants work in a job that involves regular use of the Bin-to-Bin inventory procedure. The other half of participants does not use the system for that task, and may not use the supply chain instance of PeopleSoft at all. The sample of employees represented the mix of gender in the workplace as a whole. Ethnicity, age, and education were not criterion for participation; instead, working with the complex procedure for four months or longer and using the computer daily on the job were requirements for participation. Neither was geography a criterion for participation. The number of participants from each location was random, although a balance was sought to minimize the exclusion bias effect. Since this was a new approach, there were no previous guides for sample size. Instead, the statistician recommended a minimum of 30 participants and a target of 50.

The design excluded education level for two reasons. Asking about formal education carries the risk of creating a negative feeling toward the study among some employees. Moreover, Bradley and Lee [4] found no statistically meaningful relationship between prior formal education levels and the understanding of ERP features, function, and capability.

3.1.2 Apparatus and materials

The low-complexity screen was an html high-fidelity prototype of the inventory task interface reworked into a single screen. The revision embedded process flow and supports within the interface [16], included only the needed fields, organized top-down [9], and displayed them progressively [25]. Prompts and confirming text supported the user in completing the task successfully. A mock-up and wireframe were created collaboratively with a business representative, an ERP inventory expert who understands the ERP, the business process, and user challenges. A professional web developer created the screen using the wireframe model. The reworked interface resolved two of the ERP usability errors Topi et al. [26] identified, specifically transaction execution support and overall system complexity. The low-complexity, simple screen seemed and functioned like a fully enabled PeopleSoft web page, supporting both mouse clicking and keyboard navigation.

The principal designed, built, and presented the screener questionnaire to participants using surveymonkey, a robust hosted online survey tool that exports data to Excel. Branching logic directed those providing answers based on their use of PeopleSoft.

Unattended clickstream monitoring as suggested by Babaian et al. [2] was an approach considered for this study about users working within the ERP. Collecting real-time data about thousands of inventory transfer procedures held great appeal, but was discarded for several reasons. First, the accuracy of the keyed data could not be confirmed easily. The security risks posed by running monitoring software that transmits ERP data from the production environment to a hosted server outside the firewall was another deterrent. The technical challenge of ignoring logins and passwords was another reason. These considerations, combined with the need for informed consent of study participants, meant that unattended clickstream data capture was not a viable option for this study.

All tests were conducted using a standard-issue company computer configured with Windows 7 and Internet Explorer 8. An external keyboard and a 17-inch monitor set to the standard resolution were both attached to the PC, which was hard-wired to the company network. The workstation was set up at a standing desk because this configuration was most commonly observed in the workplace. All experiments used the test instance of the web-based ERP, an identical interface with data two weeks to two months older than data in the production instance. The test environment provided the expected interface and functionality, without any risk to the business from data keyed during the experiment. The availability of data to support all scenarios was confirmed before each experimental round.

Conducting tests on the plant floor was considered, but the high probability for participants to behave differently than usual led to a decision to use a more private, enclosed room. At two sites, this was the training room. In the third, it was a small meeting room. To create a more realistic sense of the workspace, lighting was adjusted to match the normal light level on the plant floor, and an audio recording of machinery was played. A quiet lab environment is a recommendation for usability and other research [17], but in this study the lighting and audio mimicked the plant floor where the transaction is normally performed for greater environmental validity.

The principal decided not to make video recordings of participants to minimize stress and discomfort. Instead, WebEx was used to capture participant interactions with the screens and to record participant comments as they worked.

3.1.3 Protocol
A standard protocol guided the principal in leading each lab session. The materials, tasks, and scenarios were piloted with representatives of both participant groups—those who do perform the Bin-to-Bin procedure for work, and those who do not, as recommended [17]. The instruments were modified with improvements. For example, scenario structure and data formatting were revised to make it easier for participants to see and access the salient information. The data collection forms changed to make note-taking easier.

3.1.4 Procedure
The experiment combined a blend of methods. The design allowed for exploration of the question about ERP interface complexity and its impact on users working in PeopleSoft. Interface complexity was the independent variable. Because it matters most to a business with an installed ERP, task success and time on task spent completing the task were the two dependent variables. Two types of users, those who perform the procedure and those who do not, were evaluated by within-subjects and between-subjects tests. Human factors talk-aloud methods were used along with interviews to collect qualitative data.

3.2 Modelling Interface Complexity
The principal used a spreadsheet to record the task steps and build a Kieras GOMS–KLM model. Scenario one from the experiment was the task analyzed using both versions of the inventory screen. The scenario read as follows: *You're running a machine and you notice there is a defect in the finished product. The process needs to be stopped. You will use the Bin-to-Bin procedure to complete a PRODHOLD. Fifty (50) items were produced incorrectly and you need to move it from production to hold and you do need to print a facesheet to place on the product you are removing.*

The principal analyzed the default Material Transfer PeopleSoft screens and the reworked simple screen. The first pass required detailing all steps for completing the scenario using each interface. Then, for each task step, the appropriate operators were applied and their associated times calculated. The principal reviewed the composite task lists three times over several days to verify that the results of the GOMS-KLM analysis remained the same.

The principal then printed all screens used in the GOMS-KLM analysis. There were six printouts for the default interface and one for the reworked version. The researcher counted the objects and horizontal and vertical alignments on each of the printouts. The counts were repeated several times to ensure the same results were obtained each time. The principal tabulated visual complexity counts for all of the screens for each interface. The common elements and alignments from both screens were excluded from the final counts because unique measures established the difference between the complexities of the two screens used in the experiment.

4. RESULTS
ERP interface complexity was not significantly related to participant task success when using either version of the material transfer interface. Complexity was a significant factor in the time a participant spent working on the task and complexity predicted time on task. Calculations from two human factors models demonstrated that the default, complex screen had nearly twice the number of steps for the same task, and was seven times as visually complex as the simple screen.

4.1 Experiment Findings
Results from the experiment focused on the degree to which users were or were not successful, and the time each spent completing the task while working with each version of the interface. Previous studies of ERP users suggest that three variables might confuse the results about the effects of ERP user task performance: self-efficacy, years using PeopleSoft, and number of procedures keyed weekly. Consequently, the principal controlled these variables in the experiment to help ensure reliable results.

4.1.1 Task success
A task was successful when participants keyed data accurately and made correct selections before clicking the Save button. More participants succeeded in completing the task using the simple screen than the complex version of the interface. This was not a significant finding, however, for the study sample.

Participant success in using the simple interface was somewhat related to their self-efficacy (p = 0.48) or sense of confidence using technology. The years a participant had used PeopleSoft and the number of procedures keyed weekly were not related to task success, for either the complex or simple version of the interface.

Task success by participants using either screen depended upon accurate data entry in all cases. The principal observed that the participants who successfully completed the material transfer task scanned their choices to verify data accuracy before clicking Save.

4.1.2. Task time
Interface complexity was a predictor of time on task (p < .001). The more complex the interface, the more time participants needed to complete the transaction.

4.1.3. Possible significant effect
Although age was not a variable of interest, in studies of human subjects, age can emerge as significant. Whether participants were successful or not was very dependent on age in this study, particularly with the respect to use of the complex screen. Probability of success increased 15-16 times for the participants aged 45 years and younger when working with the default interface.

4.2 Interface complexity measures
Human factors task analysis and interface assessment models were used to differentiate the complex and the simple inventory screens used in the experiment. An analysis of the two screens using the Kieras GOMS-KLM model generated task-based measures. Analysis using the Galitz model generated measures for visual complexity of each interface. The results are summarized in Table 1.

The visual complexity and GOMS-KLM analyses illustrate how the default interface was 700% more complex than the simple version. The default PeopleSoft™ screens required the ERP user to complete more steps and required more thought than the simple, redesigned version. With the default interface, users completed nearly twice as many steps as they did in working with the simple screen. Almost half the steps in the complex version required mental operators of thinking and choosing, which are more challenging. The complex inventory screen was seven times as dense as the reworked simple task screen.

The simple screen decreased performance load by reducing the number of screens and on-screen elements. The simpler version required the user to complete fewer steps overall and offered fewer choice types. Together, GOMS-KLM and visual complexity measures quantified the relative concepts of simple and complex for the two interfaces, from the user's perspective.

5 LIMITATIONS
Attention was constant to issues of validity and reliability, though limitations do exist. A larger sample size would have increased the strength of the results. Remote testing might be the best means to reach additional participants in a business setting.

Testing employees who are not used to participating in experiments might have introduced unintended effects. The Hawthorne effect sees enhanced performance when participants know they are being studied. The risk for participants in this study would have been poor performance caused by stress. Anticipating a potential bias, adjustments to the protocol were made to minimize a stress effect. A stress effect among participants might have remained, however, by having a person nearby watching the participant work on the task, especially among those participants who struggled. Automated collection of task data might help mitigate these effects.

Both of the complexity modelling exercises could have been strengthened had multiple reviewers analyzed and discussed the results together. The time constraints and schedule challenges among the business team members saw the principal researcher undertake this work alone.

The experiment outcomes might have been different had a brief training been included at the outset of the experiment. Training was excluded because a test of whether or not participants could use either interface version to complete the task without training was a component of the broader research investigation. In addition, the protocol omitted training to minimize fatigue among participants and to keep the length of the session to an acceptable timeframe of thirty minutes.

Despite these limitations, the results of the research suggest possible actions for those vested in ERP systems including businesses, ERP vendors, and ERP researchers.

Table 1. Descriptive Calculations for Complex and Simple Versions of the Inventory Procedure

	GOMS KLM's				Visual Complexity*				
	Total Steps	Time Est	% Mental	% Action	Total Screens	Count Objects	C_{Horiz}	C_{Vert}	Density
Simple Version	18	25 sec	26%	74%	1	27	17	4	48
Complex, Default Screens	37	54 sec	49%	51%	6	211	94	34	339
Relative complexity of the default screen	206%	216%	188%	69%	600%	781%	553%	850%	706%

Excludes the 62 objects and counts for the default menu and top-level links in the PeopleSoft interface common to both the simple and complex interfaces.

6 DISCUSSION

In this research, ERP usability was assessed as a function of a user's ability to successfully complete a task using either the complex or a simple version of the material transfer interface. Two human factors models helped quantify ERP complexity, visually and cognitively.

Participants in the experiment could more easily complete the inventory transfer procedure using the simple screen. The redesigned interface for the inventory task was seven times simpler than the default PeopleSoft inventory screens. Progressive display of options helped direct sequential task completion by presenting needed fields at their point of use. Almost 80% of the steps required to use the redesigned screen were actions at the cursor location. The user clicked and chose, rather than thinking about what to choose or do next. Participants commented 19 times that the redesigned screen was "easy," "straightforward," or "logical." On-screen prompts and confirmations were embedded in the interface. Participants noted and commented that their data entries were "confirmed" and "verified." Drop-down lists of available options were appreciated as alternates to performing a multi-step lookup: "Getting used to drop-down's. Nice. Easier than lookup's. Like not having to manually type so I can just pick instead."

Although it was not statistically significant, the complexity of the interface did affect the users' experience in working with the screens to complete the material transfer task. The left-to-right layout of fields on the default screen suggested a different flow than the success path of up-down-across. Participants commented upon the disconnect: "You think you'd go in order", and, "I should be able to sequentially go from one thing to the next." The input fields on the default screen lacked supporting text, further complicating successful navigation and data entry. A participant lamented, before exceeding the allowed time to complete the task, "I don't know what to do or where to go." Participants wanted to succeed in their work and wanted on-screen assists and confirmation: "It should tell you if you try to put something in a bin that has something in it."

The observation that all participants who succeeded had checked their data before submitting it was a notable, unplanned finding. Scanning before saving work is a teachable, learnable behavior that was a success factor in this study.

The results of this research argue for ERP interface customizations for two reasons: enhanced usability and changes in technology. The default, complex interface contained unnecessary and non-sequential elements that prevented users from completing the inventory task. There was a clear preference for the simpler redesigned version of the screen. Some participants who were more technically proficient explained they customized the task screen using the existing interface option to enhance their own usability and efficiency. Novices too would benefit from having only necessary elements and a clear navigation path. A business gains when the ERP is used correctly, more consistently. Second, interface changes may inadvertently be introduced as dynamic web pages fill wider computer displays. A significant button on the default screen extended beyond the user's field of view with a wide screen display, though would have been more visible with a lower-resolution display

Finally, modelling the concept of complexity from the user's perspective with GOMS-KLM's and visual complexity calculation provides a measure that business implementation team members and software vendors can use to assess the usability of a system and its interface during the design phase, instead of waiting for acceptance testing or go live.

7 CONCLUSION

This research reprised 1980's and 90's human factors approaches to assess the significance of ERP interface complexity on users' ability to complete tasks successfully. An ERP representative defined ERP usability as "Your perception of how consistent, efficient, productive, organized, easy-to-use, intuitive, and straightforward it is to accomplish tasks within a system" (McGee, 2004). The premise of this research holds that successful use of the ERP, not user perception about ease of use, adoption, or satisfaction, is the more meaningful measure a business needs to assess.

Is data more accurately keyed when ERP users say of the interface, "That was easy; everything was in order"? Are there more errors when ERP users complain, "I feel stupid" because the interface is overly complex, or, lacks support for task completion? These questions are relevant to businesses. Simplified, single-screen overlays may support more consistent, successful ERP use.

Just as prototypes help the software design process, quantifying complexity helps communicate the challenges that users encounter in working with the ERP interface or how one interface is more usable than another. Further insights about the value or limits of GOMS-KLM and visual complexity models could be expected by having business laypersons apply the human factors tools from this research to other procedures and ERP systems. Assessing the outcomes of those efforts in terms of business decisions and user experience would be of interest to the information systems and human factors fields

Until these questions are answered, teaching ERP users to scan keyed data before saving is a replicable, teachable behavior observed in this research that directly contributed to task success in all cases.

REFERENCES

[1] Arnowitz, J., Gray, D., Dorsch, N., Heidelberg, M., and Arent, M. (2005). The stakeholder forest: Designing an expenses application for the enterprise. *CHI2005 Design Expo*. 941-956.

[2] Babaian, T. Lucas, W., and Topi, H. (2007) A data-driven design for deriving usability metrics. ICSOFT 2007 - International Conference on Software and Data Technologies.

[3] Bagchi, K. and Dasgupta, S. (2003). Modeling use of enterprise resources planning systems: A path analytic study. *European Journal of Information Systems*. 12(2), 142-158.

[4] Bradley, J. and Lee, C.C. (2007). ERP Training and user satisfaction: A case study. *International Journal of Enterprise Information systems*. 3(4), 33-50.

[5] Calisir, F. and Calisir, F. (2004). The relation of interface usability characteristics, perceived usefulness, and perceived ease of use to end-user satisfaction with enterprise resource planning (ERP). *Computers in Human Behavior*. 20(4), 505-515.

[6] Card, S. K., Moran, T. P., and Newell, A. (1983). *The Psychology of Human-Computer Interaction*. CRC Press Reprint.

[7] Davis, F. D. (1989). Perceived usefulness, perceived ease of use, and user acceptance of information technology. *MIS Quarterly*. 13(3), 319-340.

[8] Esteves, J.M. and Pastor, J.A. (1999). An ERP life-cycle-based research agenda. Enterprise Management and Resource Planning: Methods, Tools and Architectures EMRPS. Venice, Italy.

[9] Galitz, W.O. (1994). *It's Time to Clean your Windows: Designing GUI's that Work*. John Wiley & Sons, Inc.

[10] Holleis, P., Otto, F., and Schmidt, A. (2007). Keystroke-level model for advanced mobile phone interaction. Proceedings, Models of Mobile Interaction. April 28-May 3. San Jose, CA.

[11] Iansiti, M. (2007). ERP end-user business productivity: A field study of SAP & Microsoft. Keystone Strategy. Retrieved January 30, 2011 from http://download.microsoft.com/download/4/2/7/427edce8-351e-4e60-83d6-28bbf2f80d0b/KeystoneERPAssessmentWhitepaper.pdf.

[12] John, B. and Kieras, D. E. (1996). The GOMS family of user interface analysis techniques: Comparison and contrast, *ACM Transactions on Computer-Human Interaction*. 3(4), 320-351.

[13] Kelley, H. (2001). Attributional analysis of computer self-efficacy. Dissertation. School of Business Administration, University of Western Ontario.

[14] Kieras, D.E. (1994). GOMS modeling of user interfaces using NGOMSL. Tutorial Notes. CHI'94 Conference on Human Factors in Computer Systems. Boston, MA. April 24-28, 1994.

[15] Kieras, D.E. (2001). Using the keystroke-level model to estimate execution times. University of Michigan. Unpublished paper.

[16] Kristiansen, R. (2006). Tailoring of ERP user interfaces using an model-based approach. Unpublished. Department of Computer and Information Science, Norwegian University of Science and Technology.

[17] Lazar, J., Feng, J.H., and Hochheiser, H. (2010). *Research Methods in Human-Computer Interaction*. John Wiley & Sons, Ltd.

[18] Liu, Y., Feyen, R., and Tsimhoni, O. (2006). Queueing network-model human processor (QN-MHP): A computational architecture for multitask performance in human-machine systems. *ACM Transactions on Computer-Human Interaction*. 13(1), 37–70.

[19] Mayhew, P. (2005). Keystroke level modeling as a cost-justification tool. In Bias, R.G. and Mayhew, D.J., *Cost-Justifying Usability*. Chapter 16. Elsevier, Inc. Kindle edition.

[20] McGee, M. (2004). Master usability scaling: magnitude estimation and master scaling applied to usability measurement. *CHI 2004* April 24-29. 6(1), 335-342.

[21] Nah, F.F., Tan, X., and Teh S.H. (2004). An empirical investigation on end-users' acceptance of enterprise systems. *Information Resources Management Journal*. 17(3), 32-53.

[22] Parks, N.E. (2011). Assessing ERP usability: A user-centered and business-focused approach. Thesis. Department of Information Design & Corporate Communication, Bentley University.

[23] Saitwal, H. Feng, X., Walji, M., Patel, V. and Zhang, J. (2010). Assessing performance of an electronic health record (EHR) using cognitive task analysis. International Journal of Medical Informatics. 79(7), 501-506.

[24] Scherer, E. (2005). Results of the ERP user satisfaction survey: Conclusion for the real-world scheduling. i2s GmbH, Zurich. www.hops-research.org/.../M10_62_108200521387xzhhtjyqncedrxz.pdf.

[25] Suchman, L.A. (2007). *Human-machine Reconfigurations*. Second edition. Cambridge University Press. Kindle edition.

[26] Topi, H., Lucas, W., and Babaian, T. (2005). Usability issues with an ERP implementation. In Proceedings of the International Conference on Enterprise Information Systems. (ICEIS- 2005), 128–133.

[27] Tullis, T.S. and Albert, B. (2008). *Measuring the User Experience: Collecting, analyzing, and presenting usability metrics*. Morgan Kaufman Publishers. Kindle version.

[28] Venkatesh, V & Davis, F.D. (1996). A model of the perceived ease of use: development and test. Decision Sciences. 27(3), 451–481.

[29] Wood, S.D. and Kieras, D.E. (2002). Modeling human error for experimentation, training, and error tolerant design. The Interservice/Industry Training, Simulation & Education Conference (I/ITSEC).

[30] Yeh, J.Y. (2006). Evaluating ERP performance from the user perspective. IEEE Asia-Pacific Conference on Services Computing (APSCC'06). IEEE Computer Society.

[31] Wilcocks, L.P. and Sykes, R. (2000). Enterprise resource planning: the role of the CIO and it function in ERP. *Communications of the ACM*. 43(4), 32-38.

[32] Wu, J.H. and Wang, Y.M. (2007). Measuring ERP success: The key-users' viewpoint of the ERP to produce a viable IS in the organization. *Computers in Human Behavior*. 23(3), 1582-1596.

ACKNOWLEDGEMENTS

I thank my advisor Dr. Terrance Skelton for his guidance and generous support with the research and the thesis process. My appreciation and gratitude extend to Bentley University's Human Factors in Information Design faculty members. They inspired this thesis through rigorous coursework that provided experience as it developed an appreciation for user-centered design including iteration, tools, and user testing.

A Simulation-based Fuzzy Multi-attribute Decision Making for Prioritizing Software Requirements

Abdel Ejnioui
Information Technology
University of South Florida
Lakeland, Florida USA
1-863-667-7708
aejnioui@usf.edu

Carlos E. Otero
Information Technology
University of South Florida
Lakeland, Florida USA
1-863-667-7876
ctoero@usf.edu

Luis D. Otero
Systems Engineering
Florida Institute of Technology
Melbourne, Florida USA
1-321-674-7173
lotero@fit.edu

ABSTRACT
It is well known that most of the approaches proposed in recent research to prioritize software requirements have not been widely adopted. These approaches are too complex and time consuming, or inconsistent and difficult to implement. This paper proposes a new approach to prioritize requirements that is practical and easily implementable. Whereas most proposed approaches quantify requirements in precise and crisp parameters, this paper takes in consideration the imprecise nature of requirements by modeling their attributes as fuzzy variables. As such, these variables are integrated into a fuzzy multi-attribute decision making problem in which the requirements represented as attributes are ranked via the expected value operator of a fuzzy variable. The expected values of the attributes in the problem are computed by numerical simulation. This approach is easily extendable to include other attributes and can be easily customized as a decision making tool for software project managers.

Categories and Subject Descriptors
D.2.1 [**Software Engineering**]: Requirements/Specifications – *Tools*.

General Terms
Algorithms, Measurement, Design, Theory.

Keywords
Software quality, requirements prioritization, multi-attribute decision making, fuzzy simulation, expected operator

1. INTRODUCTION
As information technology penetrates every aspect of daily life, software engineering is becoming a vital discipline for creating software that meets customer expectations. This discipline faces numerous challenges considering the degree to which software products have evolved. In most software projects, there is a diversity of stakeholders who have vested interest in seeing their requirements included in the final deliverables of the product. These stakeholders can be users, customers, project managers, product managers, developers and testers.

Because of their positions in the software engineering process, these stakeholders formulate requirements that address their immediate sphere of concern. As a result, these requirements can be numerous, diverse in nature, may consume various amounts of resources, bring different benefits and impose different costs [1, 2]. To make matter worse, many of these requirements impose conflicting demands on software projects. Considering these requirements with their budgets in resources and times, it is not unreasonable to expect that these requirements will have different priorities. In practice, stakeholders have to find approaches by which these requirements are prioritized. Only requirements with high priorities can be implemented in earlier releases while requirements with lower priorities are can left out to late releases [3].

For some time, many attempts have been made to find effective ways to prioritize software requirements [3-5]. Some methods proposed for requirement prioritization are qualitative in nature [6, 7]. These methods rely mostly on the direct qualitative assessment of stakeholders or indirect assessment from experts who collected data from stakeholders. Although these methods can prioritize requirements in efficient ways, they fail to reveal the differences in priorities between the requirements [3]. Others have proposed quantitative methods for prioritizing requirements that can be quite effective [5, 8-11]. While some of these quantitative methods can display a high degree of consistency, they tend to be complex and impractical [12]. On the other hand, there are several quantitative methods that are informal and easy to adopt, but lack structure and consistency [13-15].

Although quantitative methods attempt to overcome the subjective nature of qualitative methods, they nevertheless suffer from the need to use precisely measureable parameters in order to prioritize software requirements. In reality, requirements are rarely quantified in precise values. This is particularly true for quality requirements, which are often vague and intangible [16, 17]. In this context, it would be reasonable to approach the challenge of requirement prioritization using fuzzy quantities instead of using crisp values. To this end, the theory of fuzzy sets can provide a number of mathematical means by which requirements can be expressed in fuzzy ways and still allow the derivation of proven methods for prioritizing requirements.

This paper proposes a novel approach for prioritizing software requirements based on the formulation of a fuzzy multiple attribute decision-making problem. Rooted in credibility theory, this approach relies on the expected value method for computing the priorities of each requirement. The remainder of this paper is as follows. Section 2 provides a summary of previous approaches for prioritizing requirements. Section 3 provides several concepts in credibility theory. Section 4 explains how the expected value operator can be used to rank fuzzy variables. Section 5 describes the formulation of the problem. Section 6 provides the proposed solution to address this problem formulation. Section 7 concludes the paper by providing a conclusion and future directions of this work.

2. RELATED WORK

As software has become more complex, and project managers are forced to make concessions and trade-offs to complete projects on schedule, requirements prioritization has become an increasingly important part of ensuring the success of a project. There are many compelling arguments as to why requirements prioritization is necessary. One of the most compelling is made by Kriegers. He argues that limited resources inevitably mean that some requirements cannot be implemented, and that the decisions about which requirements are the most important are better made in early development stages rather than in "emergency mode" towards the end of a project [5].

Most requirements prioritization methods involve examining requirements through the framework of benefit and cost [2, 12, 13]. In other words, requirements are analyzed on the basis of how much benefit that fulfilling the requirement will provide to the customer, as well as any costs associated with its implementation. This information is then used in some manner to rank the requirements in terms of their importance.

There are a number of methods that currently exist for approaching requirements prioritization. Many of these methods are quantitative, and employ a very systematic approach to gathering data and assigning values to various factors associated with requirements in order to compute a priority [2]. Other methods rely on making somewhat informal generalizations and groupings before trying to assign priorities. This is typically done to reduce the amount of time necessary to compute priorities, but may sacrifice some consistency [18].

One of the most consistent methods that have been developed is the Analytic Hierarchy Process (AHP) [19-21]. All possible pairs of requirements are enumerated, and then the perceived importance of each requirement is ranked in relationship to its pair. The most important requirement from each pair is assigned a value, while the requirement of lesser importance is given the reciprocal of that value. The redundancy of AHP does produce consistent requirements; however it also makes the process impractical for all but small projects [3, 12].

Several other methods employ a variation of the pair-wise comparisons performed for AHP. Hierarchy AHP is the most closely related; the process is nearly identical to AHP, except that requirements are first subjectively prioritized as low, medium, or high. Pair-wise comparisons are then performed on the requirements of each group [4]. Other algorithms, such as a binary search tree, and bubble-sort have also been used to compare requirements in pairs. With the exception of bubble sort, these methods require fewer comparisons than AHP. However they are still not feasible for larger projects, nor do they provide the same level of consistency [4, 9].

Total Quality Management (TQM) and Quality Function Deployment (QFD) are two other quantitative methods used to prioritize requirements. TQM ranks requirements against a set of criteria that have been deemed necessary for the success of a project [8]. A priority rank is then determined based on the weight of the success criteria and the requirement. QFD correlates the value a proposed product feature has to a customer

with specific requirements in order to determine priority. These methods are regarded as robust, however it is well known that the time and commitment needed to execute them has prevented their wide-scale adoption by organizations [8].

Despite the myriad of methods that have been proposed, research suggests that none have gained universal acclaim, nor have they been widely adopted [3]. While some methods like AHP, QFD, and TQM seem to produce more consistent prioritizations [8, 12], they are also complex, time-consuming, and difficult to implement [8]. Other less formal methods may save time initially, but could cause problems in the later stages of a project if appropriate factors are not accounted for. Lehtola's study on the practical challenges of requirement prioritization methods suggests that project managers do not have access to a method that is both simple *and* effective [22]. In order to increase the effectiveness of requirements prioritization, new methods need to be developed that save time, yet preserve the accuracy that more robust methods currently offer.

One of the latest works to propose a solution to the requirement prioritization problem is presented in [23]. In this work, the authors present a binary valued approach for prioritizing requirements that fuses benefits and costs of each requirement to provide a holistic approach to prioritization. Specifically, once requirements are elicited, a set of quality attributes is identified as evaluation criteria. These attributes are defined in terms of many different features, where each feature is determined to be present or not. Once all features are identified, each requirement is evaluated against each feature using a simple binary scale (i.e., 0 or 1). Requirements that satisfy the highest number of features would expose a higher level of quality (or priority) for that particular quality attribute. Once all requirements are evaluated and measurements computed for all features, the approach used desirability functions to fuse all measurements into one unified value that is representative of the overall quality of the requirement. This unified value is computed by using a set of desirability functions that take into consideration the priority of each quality attribute. Therefore, the resulting priority of each requirement is derived from decision-makers' goals for a specific software project. While this approach is practical and quite easy to implement, it is too simplistic since it accounts only for the presence (value 1) or absence (value 0) of features in quality attributes. In reality, information about features related to quality attributes is imprecise and in most cases incomplete.

3. PRELIMINARIES

This section introduces basic concepts in credibility theory that are critical in developing the approach proposed in this paper. Most of these concepts have been published in [21-23].

3.1 Credibility Space

Let Θ be a nonempty set and $P(\Theta)$ its power set. Each element in $P(\Theta)$ is called an *event*. The credibility of an event A, denoted by $\mathrm{Cr}\{A\}$, is a number that represents the credibility that A will occur. To insure that $\mathrm{Cr}\{A\}$ has certain mathematical properties, the following axioms must be admitted:

Axiom 1. (*Normality*) $\mathrm{Cr}\{\Theta\} = 1$.

Axiom 2. (*Montonocity*) $\mathrm{Cr}\{A\} \leq \mathrm{Cr}\{B\}$ whenever $A \subset B$.

Axiom 3. (*Self-Duality*) $\mathrm{Cr}\{A\} + \mathrm{Cr}\{A^c\} = 1$ for any event $A \in P(\Theta)$ where A^c is the set complement of A.

Axiom 4. (*Maximality*) $\mathrm{Cr}\{\cup_i A_i\} = \sup_i \mathrm{Cr}\{A_i\}$ for any events $\{A_i\}$ with $\sup_i \mathrm{Cr}\{A_i\} < 0.5$.

38

Definition 1 The set function Cr is called a *credibility measure* if it satisfies the normality, monotonocity, self-duality and maximality axioms.

Definition 2 Let Θ be a nonempty set, $P(\Theta)$ the power set of Θ, and Cr a credibility measure. Then the triplet $(\Theta, P(\Theta), Cr)$ is called a *credibility space*.

3.2 Fuzzy Variables and Credibility Distributions

Definition 3 A *fuzzy variable* is defined as a (measurable) function from a credibility space $(\Theta, P(\Theta), Cr)$ to the set of real numbers.

Theorem 1 (*Credibility Inversion*) Let ξ b a fuzzy variable with membership function μ. Then for any set B of real numbers, we have

$$\text{Cr}\{\xi \in B\} = \frac{1}{2}\left(\sup_{x \in B} \mu(x) + 1 - \sup_{x \in B^c} \mu(x)\right) \quad (1)$$

where B^c is the complement set of B. The proof of this theorem can be found in [24, 25].

Definition 4 The *credibility distribution* $\Phi: \mathbb{R} \longrightarrow [0,1]$ of a fuzzy variable ξ is defined by

$$\Phi(x) = \text{Cr}\{\theta \in \Theta \mid \xi(\theta) \leq x\}$$
$$= \frac{1}{2}\left(\sup_{y \leq x} \mu(y) + 1 - \sup_{y > x} \mu(y)\right),$$
$$\forall x \in \mathbb{R} \quad (2).$$

3.3 Expected Value

In this section, we introduce the expected value operator of a fuzzy variable. Although there are many ways to define an expected value operator, we choose to focus on the most general definition of this operator [24-26]. This definition is applicable to both continuous and discrete fuzzy variables [24].

Definition 5 Let ξ be a fuzzy variable. Then the expected value of ξ is defined as

$$E[\xi] = \int_0^{+\infty} \text{Cr}\{\xi \geq r\}dr - \int_{-\infty}^0 \text{Cr}\{\xi \leq r\}dr \quad (3)$$

provided that at least one of the two integrals is finite.

Remark 1 Let ξ and η be independent fuzzy variables with finite expected values. Then for any numbers a and b, we have

$$E[a\xi + b\eta] = aE[\xi] + bE[\eta] \quad (4).$$

This property is called the linearity of expected value operator of fuzzy variables.

3.4 Ranking of Fuzzy Variables

Contrary to the set of real numbers, fuzzy variables do not have a natural order in a fuzzy world. As such, several approaches were devised to rank fuzzy variables [27, 28]. One approach is based on the expected value operator of a fuzzy variable [26].

Definition 6 (*Expected Value Criterion*) Let ξ and η be fuzzy variables with finite expected values. We say $\xi > \eta$ if and only if $E[\xi] > E[\eta]$ where E is the expected value operator of a fuzzy variable.

4. EXPECTED VALUE OF A FUZZY VECTOR

This section introduces fuzzy simulation as a possible technique to compute the expected value of a fuzzy vector based on its credibility.

Definition 7 (α-level set) Let ξ be a fuzzy variable such that $\xi: \Theta \longrightarrow [0,1]$, μ_ξ its membership function and Θ as defined above. An α-level set of ξ where $\alpha \in [0,1]$ is defined as

$$^\alpha\xi = \{\theta \in \Theta \mid \mu_\xi(\theta) \geq \alpha\}.$$

Definition 7 Let $f: \mathbb{R}^n \longrightarrow \mathbb{R}$ be a function, and $\xi_1, \xi_2, \ldots, \xi_n$ fuzzy variables on the credibility space $(\Theta, P(\Theta), Cr)$. Then $\xi = f(\xi_1, \xi_2, \ldots, \xi_n)$ is a fuzzy variable defined as

$$\xi(\theta) = f(\xi_1(\theta_1), \xi_2(\theta_2), \ldots, \xi_n(\theta_n))$$

for any $\theta \in \Theta$.

Definition 8 An *n-dimensional fuzzy vector* is defined as a function from a credibility space $(\Theta, P(\Theta), Cr)$ to the set of n-dimensional real vectors.

Theorem 2 The vector $(\xi_1, \xi_2, \ldots, \xi_n)$ is a fuzzy vector if and only if $\xi_1, \xi_2, \ldots, \xi_n$ are fuzzy variables.

The proof of this theorem can be found in [24, 25]. Assume that x is a decision vector, $\boldsymbol{\xi}$ is a fuzzy vector and $f(x, \boldsymbol{\xi})$ is a return function. We are interested in computing the uncertain function $U: x \longrightarrow E[f(x, \boldsymbol{\xi})]$. As the expected value of a fuzzy vector, this function can be used to solve fuzzy multiple attribute decision problems using ranking criteria based on the expected values of fuzzy variables [25].

4.1 Computing the Expected Value of a Fuzzy Vector

Suppose $\xi = (\xi_1, \xi_2, \ldots, \xi_n)$ is a fuzzy vector with membership function μ while f is a function. We can generate a fuzzy simulation to compute the expected value $E[f(\xi)]$. To do so, we randomly generate u_k from the α-level sets of ξ for $k = 1, 2, \ldots, N$ where α is a small number while N is a large number. Then for any numbers $r \geq 0$, the credibility values $\text{Cr}\{f(\xi) \geq r\}$ and $\text{Cr}\{f(\xi) \leq r\}$ may be estimated by using the samples obtained from random generation of N values of r. Then, we can use simulation to calculate the expected values as [25]:

$$E[f(\xi)] = \int_0^{+\infty} \text{Cr}\{f(\xi) \geq r\}dr - \int_{-\infty}^0 \text{Cr}\{f(\xi) \leq r\}dr \quad (5)$$

4.2 Fuzzy Simulation of the Expected Value

The estimation above can be used to design the simulation algorithm described below [29]. Let $\xi = (\xi_1, \xi_2, \ldots, \xi_n)$ be a fuzzy vector and $f: \mathbb{R}^n \longrightarrow \mathbb{R}$ be a function. The expected value $E[f(\xi)] = E[f(\xi_1, \xi_2, \ldots, \xi_n)]$ can be estimated using the following algorithm:

```
Set E = 0.
Generate randomly each u_ij from the α-level sets
of ξ_1, ξ_2,...,ξ_n for i = 1, 2, ..., m and j = 1, 2, ..., n.
This generates the matrix U = [u_ij]_mxn. We denote by
u_i = (u_i1, u_i2,..., u_in) the ith row vector in U.
For each row in U
        compute f(u_i) for i = 1, 2, ..., m.
EndFor
Set a = min f(u_i) for i = 1, 2, ..., m.
Set b = max f(u_i) for i = 1, 2, ..., m.
```

```
For 1 to N
      Generate randomly r from [a, b].
      If r ≥ 0
            Set E = E + Cr{f(ξ) ≥ r}.
      ElseIf r < 0 then
            Set E = E − Cr{f(ξ) ≥ r}.
      EndIf
EndFor
Set      E[f(ξ₁, ξ₂, ..., ξₙ)] = max {a, 0} + min {b, 0} + E ·  ((b −
a))/N.
```

Note that $f(u_i)$ can be computed using the membership functions of the fuzzy variables $\xi_1, \xi_2, ..., \xi_n$ as follows:

$$f(u_i) = \min_{1 \le j \le n} \{\mu_j(u_{ij}) \mid u_i = (u_{i1}, u_{i2}, ..., u_{in})\} \qquad (6).$$

5. PROBLEM FORMULATION

Let $R = \{r_1, r_2, ..., r_m\}$ and $Q = \{q_1, q_2, ..., q_n\}$ be the set of requirements and quality attributes respectively. Associated with each quality attribute q_j, $j = 1, 2, ..., n$, a set of features $F_j = \{f_1, f_2, ..., f_{k_j}\}$ where each feature f_k, $k = 1, 2, ..., k_j$, is characterized by a fuzzy number v_k. Also associated with each attribute is a fuzzy weight w_j where the set $W = \{w_1, w_2, ..., w_n\}$ is a set of weights. Our objective is to combine the fuzzy numbers of all features within an attribute resulting in a single fuzzy number. The results will be a $m \times n$ matrix of fuzzy numbers.

5.1 Combination of Feature Fuzzy Numbers

The problem of combining a set of fuzzy numbers into a single one arises when expert opinions or imprecise estimates of a given quantity can be combined in either additive or non-additive manner by means of fuzzy number representation [30]. While several techniques have been proposed to address this problem, we choose to use the simplest one called *crisp weighting*. This approach consists of assigning weights w_k to the individual fuzzy numbers. In this case, a combination rule can be applied on the fuzzy numbers of the feature set F_j as follows:

$$C_j = \sum_{k=1}^{k_j} w_k v_k \qquad (7)$$

where $\sum_{k=1}^{k_j} w_k = 1$ and C_j is the combined fuzzy number. Note that the weights used in this approach are distinct from the weights in W defined above. Although this is not the ideal approach, it does at least preserve agreement among the values in the combined fuzzy numbers [30].

5.2 Problem Matrix

After crisp weighting of the fuzzy numbers of all features in every attribute, we obtain $m \times n$ matrix of fuzzy numbers $A = [C_{ij}]_{m \times n}$ where the m rows and n columns represent requirements and attributes respectively. In addition to this matrix, we have the vector $W = [w_1, w_2, ..., w_n]$ based on the set W defined above. This formulation is known as the *fuzzy multiple attribute decision-making* problem (FMADM) [31].

6. PROPOSED SOLUTION

This section describes the solution proposed to address the FMADM problem.

6.1 Matrix Normalization

In most FMADM problems expressed in matrix form, normalization is necessary in order to transform the matrix and weight vector numbers to comparable values. In our case,

normalization is based on the expected value operator [29]. For each fuzzy number C_{ij} in A, transform this number as follows:

If C_{ij} is a benefit:

$$\eta_{ij} = \frac{C_{ij}}{\sqrt{\sum_{i=1}^{m} (E[C_{ij}])^2}} \qquad (8)$$

If C_{ij} is a cost:

$$\eta_{ij} = \frac{p_j - C_{ij}}{\sqrt{\sum_{i=1}^{m} (E[C_{ij}])^2}} \qquad (9)$$

for $i = 1, 2, ..., n$, $j = 1, 2, ..., m$, and $p_j = \max_{1 \le i \le m} \sup\{x_{ij} \mid \mu_{ij}(x_{ij}) > 0\}$. Note that both expressions use in their denominators the expected values of the fuzzy variables of each column or attribute. Also, note that the μ_i are the membership functions of the fuzzy variables representing the attributes. The obtained normalized matrix is $B = [\eta_{ij}]_{m \times n}$.

6.2 Weight Normalization

Similar to the problem matrix, the weight vector must be normalized as follows:

$$\omega_j = \frac{w_j}{\sum_{j=1}^{n} E[w_j]} \qquad (10)$$

for $j = 1, 2, ..., n$. The final normalized weight vector is $\omega = [\omega_1, \omega_2, ..., \omega_n]$.

6.3 Expected Value Method

Given a normalized matrix of fuzzy numbers and a normalized weight vector, a simple additive weighting approach can be used to compute the following m fuzzy variables as follows [29]:

$$f_i = \sum_{j=1}^{n} \omega_j \eta_{ij} \qquad (11)$$

for $i = 1, 2, ..., m$. Each fuzzy variable can be viewed as the real-value function associated with each requirement. A utility value function $E[f_i]$, $i = 1, 2, ..., m$, based on the expected value operator can be devised to rank the m fuzzy variables. This utility $E[f_i]$ can be computed using the simulation algorithm presented in section IV.2 or computed directly if the real-value function f_i is an equipossible, triangular or trapezoidal fuzzy variable. For instance, if the fuzzy variables of the attributes are triangular variables, the real-valued function f can be computed as follows if we assume $\eta_{ij} = (a_{ij}, b_{ij}, c_{ij})$ and $\omega_j = (d_j, e_j, g_j)$:

$$f_i = \left(\sum_{j=1}^{n} a_{ij} d_j, \sum_{j=1}^{n} b_{ij} e_j, \sum_{j=1}^{n} c_{ij} g_j \right) \qquad (12)$$

for $i = 1, 2, ..., m$. In this case, the utility function of f_i can be computed as:

$$E[f_i] = \frac{1}{4} \left(\sum_{j=1}^{n} a_{ij} d_j + 2 \sum_{j=1}^{n} b_{ij} e_j + \sum_{j=1}^{n} c_{ij} g_j \right) \qquad (13)$$

for $i = 1, 2, ..., m$.

6.4 Summary of the Proposed Solution

We assume that we are given a list of requirements, attributes and their features. The proposed solution to prioritize these requirements can be summarized as follows:

```
Get the fuzzy number of each feature.
For each attribute
   Apply the crisp weighting technique to
   combine the fuzzy numbers of its features.
   Derive the membership function from the
   combined fuzzy number.
EndFor
Using the derived membership functions of the
attribute, perform the fuzzy simulation
algorithm.
Normalize the problem matrix by using the
expected value of the fuzzy variables generated
by the simulation algorithm.
Apply the expected value method on the normalized
matrix.
Sort the utility functions in non-decreasing
order.
```

The requirements that have the highest values from their corresponding utility functions have the highest priority.

7. CONCLUSION

This paper presents a novel approach to prioritize requirements based on ranking fuzzy numbers expressing the importance of an attribute in a requirement using its expected value. This ranking requires the approximation of these expected values via simulation by randomly picking values in the credibility distributions of these numbers. This approach has the capacity of fusing multiple criteria and features to provide a holistic view of quality requirements. In addition, this approach can be easily extended to include other types of requirements not considered in this paper.

This approach is currently being implemented in a custom decision-making software tool that is flexible and easy to use. This tool will be used in a case study of a software project in order to study the quality of the results it produces when different scenarios of prioritization are considered.

8. REFERENCES

[1] Asaem, M., Ramzan, M., and Jaffar, A. 2010. Analysis and optimization of software requirements prioritization techniques. *International Conference on Information and Emerging Technologies* (Karachi, Pakistan, June 2010), 1-6.

[2] Azar, J., Smith, R. K., and Cordes, D. 2007. Value-oriented requirements prioritization in a small development organization. *IEEE Software*, 24, 1, (January-February 2007), 32-37.

[3] Berander, P. 2007. *Evolving Prioritization for Software Product Management*. Ph.D. Dissertation. Bleking Institute of Technology, Sweden.

[4] Karlsson, J., Wohlin, C., and Regnell, B. 1998. An evaluation of methods for prioritizing software requirements. *Information and Software Technology*, 39, 14-15, 939-947.

[5] Kriegers, K. E. 1999. First things first: Prioritizing requirements, *Software Development*, 7, 9.

[6] Laurent, P., Cleland-Huang, J. and Duan, C. 2007. Towards automated requirements triage. *International Requirements Engineering* (New Delhi, India, October 2007), 131-140.

[7] Buyukozkan, G. and Feyzioglu, O. 2005. Group decision making to better respond to customer needs in software development. *Journal of Computers and Industrial Engineering*, 48, 2 (March 2005), 427-441.

[8] Karlsson, J. 1997. Managing software requirements using quality function deployment. *Software Quality Journal*, 6, 311-325.

[9] Karlsson, J. 1996. Software requirement prioritizing. *International Conference on Requirements Engineering*, 110-116.

[10] Karlsson, J. and Ryan, K. 1997. A cost-value approach for prioritizing requirements. *IEEE Software*, 14, 5 (September/October 1997), 67-74.

[11] Mohamed, S. I., ElMaddah, I. A. and Wahba, A. M. 2008. Towards value-based requirements prioritization for software product management. *International Journal of Software Engineering*, 1, 2 (July 2008), 35-48.

[12] Hermann, A. and Daneva, M. 2008. Requirements prioritization based on benefit and cost prediction: An agenda for future research. *IEEE International Requirements Engineering Conference* (Catalunya, Spain, September 2008), 125-134.

[13] Daneva, M. and Herrmann, A. 2008. Requirements prioritization based on benefit and cost prediction: A method classification framework. *Euromicro Conference on Software Engineering and Advanced Applications* (Parma, Italy, September 2008), 240-247.

[14] Liu, X., Veera, C. S., Sun, Y., Noguchi, K. and Kyoya, Y. 2004. Priority assessment of software requirements from multiple perspectives. *Annual Conference on Computer Software and Applications* (September 2004), 410-415.

[15] Port, D., Olkov, A. and Menzies, T. 2008. Using simulation to investigate requirements prioritization strategies. *IEEE/ACM International Conference on Automated Software Engineering* (L'Aquila, Spain, September 2008), 268-277.

[16] Gaur, V. and Soni, A. 2010. An integrated approach to prioritize requirements using fuzzy decision making. *International Journal of Engineering and Technology*, 2, 4 (August 2010), pp. 320-328.

[17] Lima, D. C., Freitas, F., Campos, G., and Souza, J. 2011. A fuzzy approach to requirements prioritization. *International Conference on Search Based Software Engineering* (Szeged, Hungary, September 2011), 64-69.

[18] Perini, A., Ricca, F., Susi, A. and Bazzanella, C. 2007. An empirical study to compare the accuracy of AHP and CBRanking techniques for requirements prioritization. *International Workshop on Comparative Evaluation in Requirements Engineering* (New Delhi, India, October 2007), 23-35.

[19] Forman, E. and Gass, S. I. 2001. The analytic hierarchy process - An exposition. *Operations Research*, 49, 9, 469-486.

[20] Saaty, T. L. 1997. That is not the analytic hierarchy process. *Journal of Multi-Criteria Decision Analysis*, 6, 6, 324-335.

[21] T. L. Saaty, *The Analytic Hierarchy Process*. McGraw-Hill, 1980.

[22] Lehtola, L., Kauppinen, M. and Kujala, S. 2004. Requirements prioritization challenges in practice.

International Conference on Product Focused Software Process Improvement (Kansai Science City, Japan, 2004), 497-508.

[23] Otero, C. E., Dell, E., Qureshi, A. and Otero, L. D. 2010. A quality-based requirement prioritization framework using binary inputs," *Fourth Asia International Conference on Mathematical/Analytical Modeling and Computer Simulation* (May 2010), 187-192.

[24] Liu, B. 2006. A survey of credibility theory. *Fuzzy Optimization and Decision Making,* 5, 4, 387-408.

[25] Liu, B. 2003. *Theory and Practice of Uncertain Programming.* Physica-Verlag Heidelberg.

[26] Liu, B. and Liu, Y.-K. 2002. Expected value of fuzzy variable and fuzzy expected value models. *IEEE Transactions on Fuzzy Systems,* 10, 4 (August 2002), 445-450.

[27] Campos Ibanez, L. M. and Munoz Gonzalez, A. 1989. A subjective approach for ranking fuzzy numbers. *Fuzzy Sets and Systems,* 29, 2 (January 1989), 145-153.

[28] Gonzalez, A. 1990. A study of the ranking function approach through mean values. *Fuzzy Sets and Systems,* 35, 1 (March 1990), 29-41.

[29] Ling, Z. 2006. Expected value method for fuzzy multiple attribute decision making. *Tsinghua Science & Technology,* 11, 1 (February 2006), 102-106.

[30] Bardossy, A., Duckstein, L. and Bogardi, I. 1993. Combination of fuzzy numbers representing expert opinions. *Fuzzy Sets and Systems,* 57, 2 (July 1993), 173-181.

[31] Kahraman, C. 2008. *Fuzzy Multi-Criteria Decision-Making: Theory and Applications with Recent Developments.* Springer Science-Business Media.

Comparison of VM Deployment Methods for HPC Education

Nicholas Robison
School of Health Sciences
Purdue University
550 Stadium Mall Drive
West Lafayette, IN 47907
nrobison@purdue.edu

Thomas Hacker
Department of Computer and Information
Technology
Purdue University
401 N. Grant Street
West Lafayette, IN 47906
tjhacker@purdue.edu

ABSTRACT

Operating System virtualization has seen major adoption across many industry fields, this growth has driven penetration into more traditional settings such as high performance computing and cluster systems. Developing an effective and efficient teaching environment for virtual high performance computing systems is complicated by a wide range of virtualization systems (open source and commercial), a variety of hardware platforms, and many different storage approaches for storing and distributing virtual machine images. Coupled with the growth in virtualization is the need for reliable, high performance storage subsystems optimized for the specific performance needs of the installation. This paper describes our experiences with using virtualization for virtual high performance computing clusters for education, and compares the performance of the popular OpenNebula virtualization manager using both NFS and SSH for virtual machine image sharing. Our results show it is possible to develop an effective teaching environment using commodity desktop computers and network hardware along with open source virtualization software.

Categories and Subject Descriptors

H.4 [**Information Systems Applications**]: Miscellaneous; D.2.8 [**Software Engineering**]: Metrics—*complexity measures, performance measures*

Keywords

Virtualization, Parallel File Systems, NFS, SSH, OrangeFS

1. INTRODUCTION

Over the past several years an increasing number of corporations and academic institutions have embraced virtualization as the 'new wave' in computing. Traditional Information Technology (IT) systems have separated the functionality of systems into discrete servers or a collection of servers that comprise a *turnkey system*. While this approach was necessary due to the limited capabilities of server hardware in the past, today that limit no longer exists. Where 10 years ago systems featured single core processors with less then 256MB of RAM[12], today it's not uncommon to find servers supporting 48-cores and up to 96GB of RAM[13]. In addition, the resources needed for routine operational tasks such as intrusion detection, IP routing, and user authentication have not seen a dramatic increase in their computational intensity or storage requirements, consequently they represent excellent candidates for coalescing these functions into larger centralized systems. High performance computing based on commodity clusters have exploited the ubiquitous availability of low cost hardware, open source operating systems, and community software and now dominate the list of the Top 500 supercomputers [18]. In recent years virtualization systems have greatly closed the performance gap both in terms of CPU throughput and network latency[22], also virtualized environments hold significant promise in reducing the time to install a cluster and configuration tasks.

Over the past decade, the high performance computing community has developed *cluster installation kits* that seek to simplify the installation and management of large scale systems. The objective of a cluster kit is to deploy an operating system image custom tailored to the site and hardware to a large number (typically hundreds to thousands) of computational nodes within a high performance computing system. Although virtualization is being widely adopted for enterprise backbone systems, support for virtual high performance computing systems in cluster kits (such as OSCAR [10] and ROCKS [17]) have not kept pace with the development of new open source virtualization systems. Virtualization has great potential utility for high performance computing, since it allows users to deploy customized operating system images to computational nodes, and to improve the reliability of large-scale systems through the use of live migration and system level checkpointing. The basic paradigm for virtual HPC systems is to create a single 'golden image' to be automatically deployed to available cluster nodes. This paradigm is especially valuable as many scientific applications have very rigid library and path requirements and the ability to optimize only a single image is a huge advantage to administrators, likewise modifying a virtual image and deploying the changes is a simple task.

We have developed a hands-on approach for teaching virtual high performance computing that uses commodity hardware and open source virtualization and cloud computing software that allows students to design, build, and benchmark virtual high performance computing clusters as a part of a progressive assignment over the course of the semester. This approach uses recycled desktop computers, commodity network hardware, CentOS Linux, open source HPC libraries (e.g. MPICH2 [6]), the KVM [8] virtualization system, and the OpenNebula [5] cloud computing software.

During the course of the semester, we found that as the number of virtual cluster VM images grows, so does the need to store and quickly deploy VM images to computational nodes. We considered a number of approaches to solve this problem, with the goal in mind to find a solution that would be simple and adhere to the open source and commodity hardware approach we developed. We considered and evaluated three different approaches: Network File System (NFS) based storage; simple system-to-system copying using scp; and the use of the OrangeFS[16] parallel file system.

Our initial analysis found that each of these approaches have inherent strengths and weaknesses. To our surprise, we found no research that empirically investigates the performance differences between the three approaches. We needed a quantitative assessment to compare these three options to select the best approach for students to use in developing their virtual high performance computing clusters. In this paper, we present the results of a series of network and disk I/O tests comparing the various systems under load within a virtual high performance computing system. In the next section, we provide an overview of the experimental cluster and the various software packages used, Section 3 details our experimental methodology, the results of the benchmarks are discussed in Section 4, and Section 5 outlines our conclusions and future work.

2. CLUSTER CONFIGURATION

2.1 Hardware

For our assessment, we built a test cluster that consisted of 16 Dell Optiplex [4] computers equipped with Core2Duo 6400 processors at 2.13GHz and 2MB of cache. They also featured 2GB DDR2 RAM and a single 160GB 7200RPM Hard Drive. The cluster head node contained an additional 160GB 7200RPM Hard Drive for storing and deploying the Virtual Machine (VM) images. The nodes were divided into 4 'carts' of 4 machines each and connected via 1Gb ethernet to a Netgear GS108T network switch located on the cart. The switches were then connected with 2x1Gb ethernet links in a round-robin configuration, this was done to maximize the available bandwidth between the carts as a large non-blocking switch was not able to be procured for this experiment.

We assessed OrangeFS on a different cluster built from the identical type of hardware used for the NFS and SSH tests. We configured 10 OrangeFS server nodes, and stored a 20 GB VM image on OrangeFS. We used RHEL6 with KVM on the compute and OrangeFS nodes with networking provided by a Force-10 S50 network switch. OpenNebula

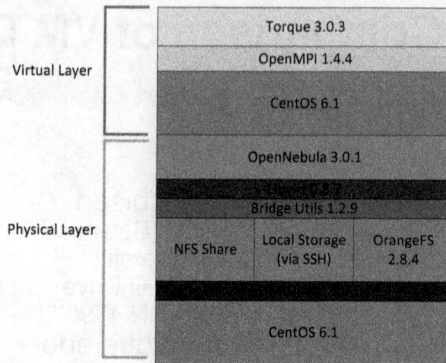

Figure 1: Cluster Software Stack

was configured to copy the VM image from the OrangeFS file system mounted on the compute node to a local disk.

Each compute node virtual hardware platform for the NFS and SSH tests were installed with CentOS Linux with KVM, and configured with a bare minimum of required packages and services that used less then 360MB of RAM in an idle state. The head node was configured with the GNOME desktop manager and hosted the OpenNebula server, as well as the DHCP server for the Virtual Machines, NFS share for the VM images, and the Cobbler [19] server used in loading the OS onto the physical nodes. The head node used nearly 756MB of RAM during idle and as such was configured to only host a single 'server' VM and was not used for any computation.

2.2 Software

The software stack for this cluster includes a series of applications in both the physical and virtual space, each is built on top of the next to provide the necessary functionality.

Hypervisor: we used the QMU-KVM hypervisor [9], which is included in the default repository and is actively supported by the community, other alternatives include the Xen Hypervisor [3] now part of the Citrix family, and VMWare vSphere[21]. We chose KVM not only because of its fully open source nature, but also its performance, when compared to Xen, and ease of installation[2].

Storage System: We implemented three different configurations: NFS share (OpenNebula default), SSH deployment, and OrangeFS [16].

NFS: This is the default OpenNebula configuration in which the VM images are hosted by the OpenNebula server and deployed to the compute nodes. This configuration provides a centralized image management scheme as well the ability to live migrate images between nodes; however, it concentrates all network disk I/O to a single node, potentially creating a major bottleneck. In addition, this deployment scheme requires the VM image to be created, loaded into the OpenNebula image repository and then replicated into a separate directory for each deployment. This means that for a 5 node cluster up to 7 copies of the same VM are stored on disk, which is a problem for virtual clusters using hundreds or thousands of nodes.

scp/SSH: An alternate configuration is to deploy the VM images over the network and store them on the local disks of the compute nodes. This has the benefit of reducing the centralized storage requirements as well as potentially increasing disk I/O performance, since each VM accesses the local disk instead of a remote NFS server. The potential downside is that all images must be initially deployed over ethernet and potentially over a single 1Gb ethernet connection, also as the VM images are stored remotely it potentially increases the management requirements of tracking the various VM versions that may be orphaned on remote machines due to a power or network outage.

OrangeFS: A potentially better solution is to implement a parallel file system underneath the OpenNebula image repository. By giving each node high speed access to a distributed file system OpenNebula can share images using a separate storage system with potentially isolated data and communication pathways. As has been seen in other studies [11] this can greatly reduce the deployment times of VMs as well as increase disk I/O performance. As an added bonus, because OpenNebula is configured to use an NFS share it maintains the ability to live migrate VMs across nodes as well as utilize a central image management scheme.

Networking: To create a seamless network between the physical and virtual nodes Bridge-Utils 1.2.9 was installed and configured, this allowed easy and rapid data transfer between VMs on discrete nodes and no significant performance decrease was noted.

Virtual Machine Management: We managed the VMs using a combination of libvirt (v0.8.7) and OpenNebula (v3.0.1) [15]. OpenNebula provided the user interface between the VM storage and deployment system and passed management commands to the libvirt package which in turn controlled the KVM hypervisor. These two packages provided seamless management and control over multiple VM images and host nodes. This allowed the user to learn a single set of OpenNebula specific commands and control a variety of different hypervisors including, KVM, Xen, VMWare, and Virtualbox. For this experiment only KVM was utilized for the sake of simplicity.

Parallel Networking: In order to support parallel network communication across the VM images OpenMPI 1.4.4 [14] was installed on the master VM image.

Job Scheduler: While manually submitting MPI jobs is an option for more experienced users it doesn't offer the robustness or automation a more full featured job scheduler, thus Torque 3.0.3 [1] was compiled and installed as well. OpenMPI natively supports integration when compiled with the appropriate flags, this configuration allows users to natively submit MPI jobs through a central queue without worrying about host files and various configurations, they simple select the program to run and the number of nodes they require, Torque does the rest.

While the software stack contains multiple overlapping and seemingly obscure packages, the end result is a single unified queue and common command interface (Torque) that any approved user can connect to and submit jobs to with the ability to live migrate VMs from congested or failing nodes (when configured with NFS or OrangeFS), the result is a robust, resilient, and easy to use computing cluster that can dynamically scale as needed. A visual overview of the entire software stack is given in Figure 1, along with a distinction between what software operates within the virtual machines and which installed on the physical nodes.

3. METHODOLOGY

For this experiment three micro benchmarks were used to test various components of system functionality, this was in addition to manually measuring standard deployment times. The details for the benchmarks used are given from the source website:

OSU Microbenchmarks multi_latency: This test is carried out in a ping-pong fashion between multiple pairs of nodes. Many iterations of this test are carried out and the average one-way latency numbers are obtained [20].

OSU Microbenchmarks multi_bandwith: This test evaluates the aggregate uni-directional bandwidth and message rates between multiple pairs of processes. The objective of this benchmark is to determine the achieved bandwidth and message rate from one node to another node with a configurable number of processes running on each node. Only the bandwidth portion of the test is presented here [20].

IOzone: This program evaluates the read, write, re-read, re-write, random read, and random write performance over large and small file sizes. Multiple iterations of test parameters were used to find the ideal configuration that would yield accurate results without requiring extremely long testing times. The final configuration tested I/O performance using 8k sectors over a 1.5GB maximum file size. This maximum was chosen as 2x the size of maximum RAM allocation, this was on recommendation from the IOzone user documentation [7].

The testing methodology is as follows; OpenNebula was configured first using standard NFS and then SSH, as the configuration change required completely redoing the host node connections the entire benchmark process was run on one method then the other. For each configuration the 'head node' image was deployed to the 'HeadNode' physical machine and was used only for hosting the various Torque and OpenMPI services, it was not used in the computational or deployment benchmarks. Next the compute node VM images were deployed in batches of two, the time between the first VM reporting PENDING, and the final machine reporting RUNNING was recorded. These times were chosen as they were the most reliable time metrics recorded by OpenNebula, additional time was required to fully boot the images and negotiate an address with the DHCP server but this was not recorded due to a lack of accuracy in the log files. Once the VMs were booted the Torque server on the 'head node' VM was configured to use the new compute nodes and the 'pbs_mom' process was started. A simple bash script was designed to run each micro benchmark 3 times alternating between the tests in a sequence of 'multi_latency' − > 'multi_bandwidth' − > 'IOzone' to avoid buffer caching. The VM images were then destroyed and after a 30 second delay the next set of VMs were deployed and the process repeated itself.

Initially the test was designed to support a maximum of 30 VMs (two per physical node) but the single hard drive in the head node was unable to support more then 10 at a time, due to both performance and space issues; thus the test was limited from its original intent.

The OrangeFS tests were performed in a similar manner and with matching methodology, but as they were performed on a separate cluster they were run independent of the NFS and SSH tests.

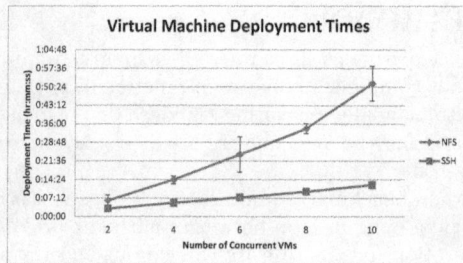

Figure 2: Deployment Times

4. RESULTS

The results of the tests are presented in the following section along with analysis of the results and conclusions as to the perceived performance. Throughout the remaining sections the OrangeFS cluster will be mentioned in contrast to the experimental cluster, but direct performance comparisons are not possible due to its installation on a cluster with different networking and OS configurations.

4.1 Deployment

Deployment times of virtual machines varied depending on the type of cluster installation. For a traditional high performance computing (HPC) cluster in which the system is never fully taken offline the time to recover a failed node is of less importance then to an installation (such as cloud computing) in which compute services are delivered in a on-demand fashion. Nevertheless, deployment is a crucial test in that it involves both the I/O and networking subsystems and as the number of concurrent VMs increases so does its stress on the available hardware.

Initially we suspected that the NFS configuration would provide the fastest deployment times as it does not require copying the images over a single ethernet connection and allows all read/write operations to take place on a single disk. Likewise the SSH deployment should be constrained by the need to push all images over a single connection and we expected to see an exponential increase in deployment times as the number of images increased. In fact, the opposite was true, as can been see in Figure 2. SSH showed only a slight, linear time increase vs the number of deployed images while NFS showed a significant (almost exponential) time increase. An explanation for this is that requiring a single disk spindle to perform simultaneous read and write operations created a 'worse case scenario' in which all operations became random in nature; deploying the images to remote machines allowed the drives to focus on a single operation in a sequential manner. Also of interest is the fact that the standard deviation bars are barely visible for the SSH graph but are pronounced for NFS.

4.2 Bandwidth

VM transfer time depends on bandwidth which is the ability to transfer large amounts of data. Scientific applications running with compact VMs also rely on bandwidth for good performance. NFS installations must share the ethernet backbone between compute node communications and VM transfers. In SSH installations all disk I/O should be constrained to the individual host nodes to facilitate higher aggregate bandwidth, especially as the VM count increases.

The NFS configuration showed large performance variabil-

ity when the VM count was greater then 6, and the standard deviation computed for NFS showed massive variance for the 8 and 10 node deployments. The standard deviation for the SSH setup was much less and is not given here. These results indicate compared with disk activity the network, does have an impact on bandwidth but only on larger installations. SSH configurations showed a much smoother

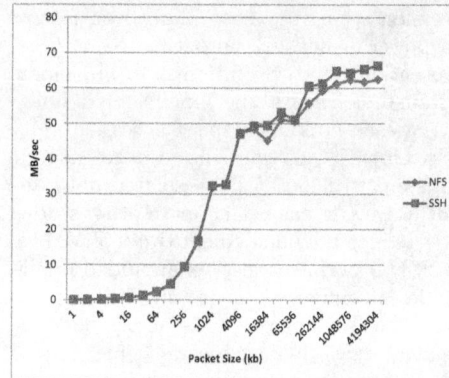

(a) SSH vs. NFS Bandwidth

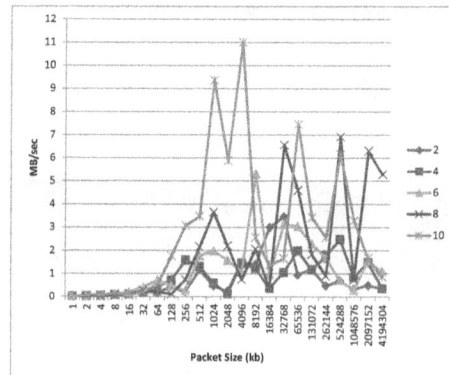

(b) NFS Standard Deviation

Figure 3: Bandwidth Tests

bandwidth curve with little deviation, further confirming the assumption that disk activity has an impact on cluster network performance; however, when the average bandwidth between SSH and NFS configurations is compared (Figure 3(a)) there is no difference until the VM number is 8 or 10 and even then the difference is not statistically significant. This shows that while disk I/O does have an impact on performance it is not significant given the size of the study (10 VMs max), if more VMs were deployed it is possible that SSH configurations would show a significant performance boost, but as of now the data does not support that conclusion. One explanation for these findings is that the micro benchmark does not write to disk and remains mostly in RAM, thus removing almost all disk I/O from the picture.

For OrangeFS, we were able to transfer a 20 GB VM image in an average of 474 seconds, yielding an effective throughput of 43.2 MB/sec. This was much higher that the 10.9 MB/sec for NFS VM image deployment and 21MB/sec for SSH. This was not surprising, since the 10-way striping we used for the OrangeFS servers provided much faster disk access than a single NFS server.

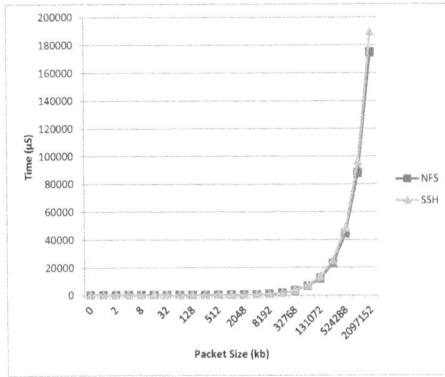

Figure 4: Average Latency Comparison

4.3 Latency

High performance computing is often dependent on extremely low latency network communications, fields such as fluid dynamics and physical collision simulation function by breaking the problem in a series of chunks that are processed by individual nodes, the results of these codes are often dependent on the results of the adjacent chunks which may not be computed on the same physical node, thus these applications are often network bound and any software package that increases overall latency or network jitter would be considered completely unfeasible. It can be suspected that the SSH installation should see lower latencies as disk I/O calls are not competing with MPI calls from the computational program; likewise, the NFS configuration should introduce significant jitter and variable performance, especially as the VM count increases.

Fortunately this does not turn out to be the case, as is seen in Figure 4 the latency between the different configurations is almost completely equal with SSH showing slightly higher latency at the larger packet sizes, but again, the results are insignificant. Also of interest is the fact that the resulting curves are extremely smooth and show almost identical response for all numbers of VMs with NFS showing slightly lower latency when only running 2 VMs, overall this shows that no significant performance difference exists between the various configurations and that VM number has little effect on overall latency, this is good news for many cluster administrators.

4.4 Disk I/O

The results of the IOzone benchmark are provided in Figure 4.4, and provide some interesting insights, for the NFS setup the standard deviation of many of the results (Figure 5(b) for example) is extremely large and in some cases extends beyond the entire range of results. An explanation of this phenomena is that the NFS configuration is extremely sensitive to network traffic, and any differences are exhibited in the final results. Of additional note is the fact that the SSH results were primarily uniform and showed small variance across any number of VM images. Plotting the average disk I/O of both installations shows that there is little statistical difference between the 2 configurations except for 'random reads', on an anecdotal note the system, when running the NFS images, exhibited major issues with many system operations timing out, and the console becoming unusable, the SSH system exhibited none of these issues and remained

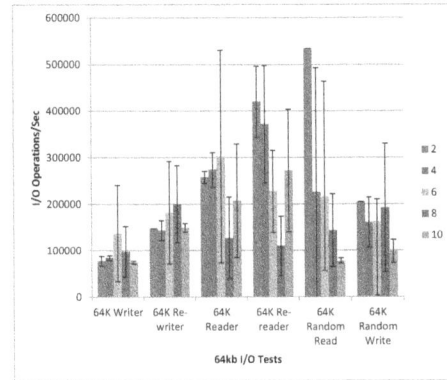

(a) NFS 64kB

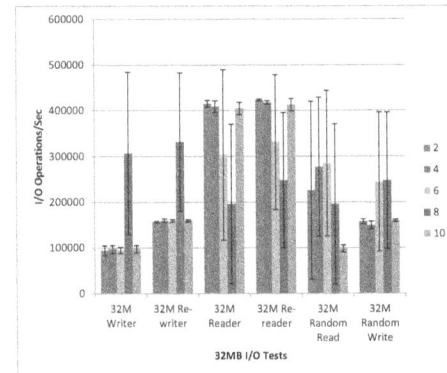

(b) NFS 32MB

usable through the tests. Our conclusions show no major performance decrease as the number of images increases, of course, with the number of VM deployments never exceeding 10 there was never more then a single VM running on any host node at one time, it remains to be seen how performance would be affected if multiple VMs were deployed to each host node.

5. CONCLUSIONS

In conclusion, while it was initially thought that an SSH system would provide significant performance benefits in all factors except deployment times, no significant differences were observed between the two configurations. What differences did exist were small and generally not statistically significant. It's important to understand that limitations are present in this experiment. First, as the single disk in the 'HeadNode' limited to a maximum of 10 running VM images with 16 host nodes in the cluster the full system performance was rarely tested and while performance hits were observed in the upper limits (8 to 10 concurrent VMs) the experiment was not large enough to truly capture and test these results. Second, the disk results returned for the NFS configuration were no fully accurate and reflected problems stemming from the lack of a robust I/O subsystem. Nevertheless, the network benchmarks showed that little difference exists between the two configurations except for the area of deployment times. Cluster administrators must balance their need to migrate running VMs from failing nodes with the ability to rapidly deploy new VM nodes on demand. When looking at the OrangeFS cluster it becomes apparent

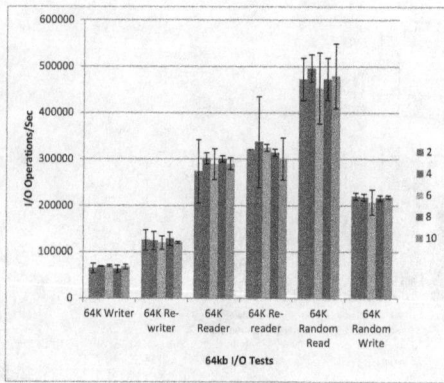

(c) SSH 64kB

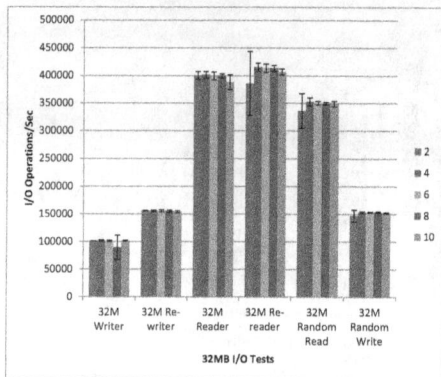

(d) SSH 32MB

Figure 5: Iozone Tests

that this has the potential to be the ideal method for rapidly deploying and maintaining multiple VM images, combining the deployment speed of SSH with the live migration capabilities of NFS; although, this comes at the cost of added complexity by involving another software package that must be supported.

Future work should focus on extending the number of concurrent VMs and replacing the single disk in the 'HeadNode' with a robust storage solution more likely to be found in a large corporate or academic setting.

This paper represents an important first step in understanding that the default OpenNebula configurations may provide a significant performance penalty as the size of the cluster grows, any administrator looking to install such a system would do well to consider all the available storage options and find that one that works best for their particular usage patterns and needs.

6. REFERENCES

[1] Adaptive Computing. orque resource manager, 2011.

[2] A. Chierici and R. Veraldi. A quantitative comparison between xen and kvm, 2010.

[3] Citrix Systems. Xen hypervisor, 2012.

[4] Dell Computer. Optiplex desktops, 2011.

[5] J. Fontán, T. Vázquez, L. Gonzalez, R. Montero, and I. Llorente. Opennebula: The open source virtual machine manager for cluster computing. In *Open Source Grid and Cluster Software Conference*, 2008.

[6] W. Gropp. Mpich2: A new start for mpi implementations. *Recent Advances in Parallel Virtual Machine and Message Passing Interface*, pages 37–42, 2002.

[7] IOzone. Iozone filesystem benchmark, 2011.

[8] A. Kivity, Y. Kamay, D. Laor, U. Lublin, and A. Liguori. kvm: the linux virtual machine monitor. In *Proceedings of the Linux Symposium*, volume 1, pages 225–230, 2007.

[9] KVM Project. Kvm project, 2011.

[10] T. Naughton, S. Scott, B. Barrett, J. Squyres, A. Lumsdaine, and Y. Fang. The penguin in the pail–oscar cluster installation tool. In *The 6th World Multi Conference on Systemics, Cybernetics and Informatics (SCI 2002)*, 2002.

[11] B. Nicolae, J. Bresnahan, K. Keahey, and G. Antoniu. efficient multideployment on clouds, 2011.

[12] T. Olivares, L. Orozco-Barbosa, F. Quiles, A. Garrido, and P. J. Garcia. Performance study of nfs over myrinet-based clusters for parallel multimedia applications. In *Electrical and Computer Engineering, 2001. Canadian Conference on*, volume 2, pages 999–1004 vol.2, 2001.

[13] Open Compute Project. Amd motherboard, 2011.

[14] Open-MPI Project. Open mpi: High performance computing, 2011.

[15] OpenNebula Project. Opennebula project, 2011.

[16] Orange File System Project. Welcome to the orange file system project, 2011.

[17] ROCK Linux. Rock linux distribution build kit, 2011.

[18] T. Site. Top500 list–november 2010 (1-100). *Top500 Supercomputing Site [Website], February*, 5, 2011.

[19] The Cobbler Project. Cobbler project, 2011.

[20] The Ohio State University. Micro-benchmarks, 2011.

[21] VMWare Corporation. Vmware vsphere, 2012.

[22] J. Walters and V. Chaudhary. A fault-tolerant strategy for virtualized hpc clusters. *Journal of Supercomputing*, 50(3):209–239, 2009.

Defining IT Research

Rob Friedman
University of Washington Tacoma
1900 Commerce St.
Tacoma, WA 98402
(001) 253-692-4611
rsfit@uw.edu

Mark Stockman
University of Cincinnati
2600 Clifton Ave.
Cincinnati, OH 45221
(001) 513-556-4227
mark.stockman@uc.edu

Han Reichgelt
Southern Polytechnic State University
1100 South Marietta Parkway
Marietta, GA 30060
(001) 678-915-7399
hreichge@spsu.edu

William W. Agresti
The Johns Hopkins Carey
Business School
100 International Dr.
Baltimore, MD 21202
(001) 410-234-9403
wagrest1@jhu.edu

Joseph J. Ekstrom
Brigham Young University
Provo, UT 84602
(001) 801-422-1839
jekstrom@byu.edu

ABSTRACT

Information Technology emerged as a separate computing discipline primarily because the computing disciplines that were taught in universities at the time, in particular computer science and information systems, did not meet the needs of employers. In particular, the existing computing disciplines did not meet employer needs for IT infrastructure managers. While IT was successful in meeting employer needs, it was slow to develop a distinct research agenda, and it has become clear that, if it is to gain credibility in an academic environment, it needs to do so.

Categories and Subject Descriptors

K.0 General

Keywords

Research, anchor theme, systems, discipline, sustainability.

1. INTRODUCTION

The goal of this panel is to provide a variety of positions statements and rationales that contribute to our community's defining a scope of research for the discipline of Information Technology. We address such questions as: What will it take to have IT recognized as a peer discipline in a computing environment populated by more established disciplines? What strategies should the discipline employ to establish a research foothold in that space? What "IT research thrust areas" [1] should IT program faculty engage to maintain and further develop the discipline?

2. POSITION 1: HAN REICHGELT

I propose two streams of research activities and discuss the challenges they present. First, the use of IT in specific application domains, such as health care or education, the extent to which insights from one application domain generalize to another, and what domain features prevent such generalizations. The second is taking place in what the Information Systems community refers to as the "practitioner literature", e.g., white papers and case studies,

often produced by IT consulting firms. Its challenge for us is to find ways to determine to what extent this stream's research results meet the higher standards of academic research.

3. POSITION 2: WILLIAM AGRESTI

A systematic scheme for crafting an IT research agenda begins by mapping IT with related disciplines in the computing space, suggesting a distinctive anchoring theme for the IT discipline such as deployment and configuration. The spatial positioning of IT helps motivate a strategic approach for defining IT research by seizing on jurisdictional vacancies, abstracting from professional practice, and drawing upon theoretical results from the systems sciences, serving as a reference discipline for IT. Resulting IT research thrust areas — IT artifacts, enterprise architectural infrastructure, interaction models, system performance, and domain induction — match well with perceived societal needs for advances in IT.

4. POSITION 3: J. EKSTROM

IT practice is increasingly involved with aggregating services provided by disparate systems into systems of systems that provide other services. One of the most difficult problems in managing the delivery of these aggregated services is fault isolation and root cause analysis during failure. These problems are compounded by the increased use of virtualization technologies that introduce functional layers with associated failures at each layer. How do we model and manage such systems? What are the security implications? Can the System of Systems work in other disciplines guide our thinking? We need to make progress or be crushed under the complexity of our success.

5. POSITION 4: MARK STOCKMAN

As a discipline not born from unanswered research questions in a related field, Information Technology (IT) struggles with a chicken and egg problem. Primary research requires doctoral students to carry out work being led by faculty, but the creation of a research-based doctoral program requires faculty with funded research. Each of the research thrusts presented in "Toward an IT Agenda" [1] seems relevant. At my own institution, a Research 1 university, domain induction may be the most practical route. IT faculty here are beginning to partner with researchers and their graduate students in areas of criminal justice, education, and political science.

6. POSITION 5: ROB FRIEDMAN

An unrealized advantage the IT community is its maturing in the Web 2.0 era, in which socio-technical systems are open in terms of access and process. As we debate content questions, we also need to pay attention to process questions, such as how and why individuals and groups exchange information to further disciplinary ends. IT research can be defined as the investigation of sustainable knowledge exchange systems design, which has the goal of reshaping not only the infrastructure, but also the methodologies and cultures of research and education by opening the door to a much wider community of participants.

7. REFERENCES

[1] Agresti, W. 2011. Toward an IT Agenda. *Communications of the Association for Information Systems*: Vol. 28, Article 17.

A Survey of SCADA and Critical Infrastructure Incidents

Bill Miller
Brigham Young University
Information Technology Program
Provo, Utah
+1 (801) 422 1985
bill_miller@byu.edu

Dale C. Rowe Ph.D
Brigham Young University
Information Technology Program
Provo, Utah
+1 (801) 422 6051
dale_rowe@byu.edu

ABSTRACT

In this paper, we analyze several cyber-security incidents involving critical infrastructure and SCADA systems. We classify these incidents based on Source Sector, Method of Operations, Impact, and Target Sector. Using this standardized taxonomy we can easily compare and contrast current and future SCADA incidents.

Categories and Subject Descriptors

C.2.0 [**Computer-Communication Networks**]: General --- Security and Protection.

General Terms

Documentation, Security.

Keywords

SCADA, Critical infrastructure, Security, Cyber security, Information assurance and security, Cyber attack, Incident response.

1. INTRODUCTION

Supervisory Control and Data Acquisition (SCADA) systems are used in many Critical Infrastructure applications. These applications are increasingly becoming the targets of cyber-attacks.

Historically, SCADA systems relied on air-gapped networks and non-standard protocols to protect them from attack. Increasingly, these networks have been connected to corporate networks and thus, the internet. There have also been advances in using standard networking protocols for communications [1].

These changes have made SCADA systems more available for attackers to target from anywhere in the world. The critical nature of these systems also makes these intriguing targets. For the first time, attacks in cyberspace can have physical manifestations in the real world. This presents a valuable and in many instances, easy to access target to those who desire to cause disruption to physical services for whatever motive. These factors have combined to increase the number of attacks against SCADA systems.

In order to prepare to defend against future attacks against critical infrastructure, it is necessary to understand how these attacks have been carried out in the past. In this paper, we will discuss a sampling of these historical attacks and classify them by factors that allow us to analyze these attacks along with their targets and sources. This analysis will allow us to more clearly understand the nature of these attacks and how they may be carried out in the future.

2. CLASSIFICATION OF INCIDENTS

For the purposes of this paper, we use a modified version of the taxonomy presented by Kjaerland to classify attacks based on 'Source Sectors', Method of Operation (MO)', 'Impact', and 'Target Sectors' [5]. Each facet of the classification can be broken down into the terms shown in Table 1 and are subsequently explained.

Table 1: Taxonomy [5]

Source Sectors	Method of Operation(MO)	Impact	Target Sectors
Com	Misuse of Resources	Disrupt	Com
Gov	User Compromise	Distort	Gov
Edu	Root Compromise	Destruct	Intl
Intl	Social Engineering	Disclosure	
User	Virus	Death	
Unknown	Web Compromise	Unknown	
	Trojan		
	Worm		
	Recon		
	Denial of Service		
	Other Sys Failure		

2.1 Source Sectors

Source of the incident if explicitly identified (all sectors refer to US sites, except Intl.).

Com – Denotes a commercial source (including consumer products, industry, small business).

Gov – Denotes local or national government (including buildings/housing, emergency services, public benefits, social services, state and federal government, taxes, tribal governments, worker protections, environment, military).

Edu – Denotes a postsecondary school.

Intl – Denotes a Non-US entity.

User – Denotes an individual user.

Unknown – Indicates the source is not known.

2.2 Method of Operation (MO)

Method(s) used by a perpetrator to carry out an attack.

Misuse of Resources – Unauthorized use of IT resources. Ex. Storing unauthorized files on a server, using site as springboard for further unauthorized activity.

User Compromise – Perpetrator gains unauthorized use of user privileges on a host.

Root Compromise – Perpetrator gains unauthorized administrator privileges on a host.

Social Engineering – Gaining unauthorized access to privileged information through human interaction and targeting people's minds rather than their computers.

Virus – A virus is a piece of code that, when run, will attach itself to other programs, which will again run when those programs are run.

Web Compromise – Using vulnerabilities in a website to further an attack.

Trojan – A Trojan is a program that adds subversive functionality to an existing program.

Worm – A program that propagates itself by attacking other machines and copying itself to them.

Recon – Scanning/probing site to see what services are available. Determining what vulnerabilities exist that may be exploited.

Denial of Service – An exploit whose purpose is to deny somebody the use of the service: namely to crash or hang a program or the entire system.

Other Sys Failure – The incident was caused by a design failure or other unknown.

2.3 Impact

The effect of an attack.

Disrupt – Access change, removal of access to victim or to information. Manipulate permissions, e.g. Denial of Service attack or Trojan horse. 'Disrupt' would be the least invasive nature of attack.

Distort – File change, modification of information from victim. This is a change to data within files.

Destruct – File deletion, removal of information from victim. Destruct would be seen as the most invasive and malicious and may include Distort or Disrupt.

Disclosure – Unauthorized exposure of information, other than in support of one of the above. Disclose would imply disclosure of information that may lead to further compromises. Ex. Download of password file.

Death – Loss of human life.

Unknown – Insufficient information to classify.

2.4 Target Sectors

Victim of the incident (all sectors refer to US sites, except Intl.).

Com – Commercial entity (including consumer products, industry, small business).

Gov – Local or national government (including buildings/housing, emergency services, public benefits, social services, state and federal government, taxes, tribal governments, worker protections, environment, military).

Intl – A Non-US target.

3. SURVEY OF INCIDENTS

The following are an analysis of several Critical Infrastructure security failings in chronological order. For each failure a brief description and classification using the aforementioned taxonomy is provided. Note that not every failure is due to external attack (although this is true for the majority).

3.1 Siberian Pipeline Explosion (1982)

This is the first known cyber-security incident involving critical infrastructure. In 1982, intruders planted a Trojan in the SCADA system that controls the Siberian Pipeline. This caused an explosion equivalent to 3 kilotons of TNT [2].

Source Sector: Unknown

MO: Trojan

Impact: Distort

Target Sector: Intl

3.2 Chevron Emergency Alert System (1992)

A fired employee of Chevron's emergency alert network disabled the firm's alert system by hacking into computers in New York and San José, California, and reconfiguring them so they would crash. The vandalism was not discovered until an emergency arose at the Chevron refinery in Richmond, California, and the system could not be used to notify the adjacent community of the release of a noxious substance. During the ten-hour period in 1992 when the system was down, thousands of people in twenty-two states and six unspecified areas of Canada were put at risk [3].

Source Sector: User

MO: Misuse of Resources, User Compromise

Impact: Disrupt

Target Sector: Com

3.3 Salt River Project (1994)

Between July 8th and August 31st, 1994, an attacker gained unauthorized access to the Salt River Project computer network via a dialup modem so he could have access to billing information. He installed a back door into the system giving him access at a later time. At the time, Salt River Project's water SCADA system operated a 131-mile canal system, which was used to deliver water to customers in the Phoenix metropolitan area. The attacker had at least one 5-hour session on mission critical systems which controlled the canals. Data vulnerable during the intrusions included water and power monitoring and delivery, financial, and customer and personal information. Data taken and/or altered included login and password files, computer system log files, and "root" privileges [11].

Source Sector: User

MO: Root Compromise, Trojan

Impact: Disclosure

Target Sector: Gov

3.4 Worcester, MA Airport (1997)

In March 1997, one hacker penetrated and disabled a telephone company computer that serviced Worcester Airport in Massachusetts. As a result, the telephone service to the Federal Aviation Administration control tower, the airport fire department, airport security, the weather service and various private airfreight companies was cut off for six hours. Later in the day, the juvenile disabled another telephone company computer, this time causing an outage in the Rutland area. The outage caused financial losses and threatened public health and public safety [3].

Source Sector: User

MO: Root Compromise, Denial of Service

Impact: Disrupt

Target Sector: Gov

3.5 Gazprom (1999)

In 1999, hackers broke into Gazprom, a gas company in Russia. The attack was collaborated with a Gazprom insider (disgruntled employee). The hackers were said to have used a Trojan Horse to gain control of the central switchboard, which controls gas flow in pipelines [8].

Source Sector: Intl

MO: User Compromise, Trojan

Impact: Disrupt

Target Sector: Intl

3.6 Bellingham, WA Gas Pipeline (1999)

In June 1999, 237,000 gallons of gasoline leaked from a 16" pipeline into a creek that flowed through Whatcom Falls Park in Bellingham, Washington. About 1 1/2 hours after the rupture, the gasoline ignited and burned approximately 1 1/2 miles along the creek causing 3 deaths and 8 documented injuries. The pipeline failure was exacerbated by control systems not able to perform control and monitoring functions. The National Transportation Safety Board (NTSB) report issued October 2002 cited one of the five key causes of the accident was the Olympic Pipe Line Company's practice of performing database development work on the SCADA system while the system was being used to operate the pipeline [10]. While not technically an attack, the loss of human life in this incident illustrates the dangers of any type of failure in a critical infrastructure system.

Source Sector: User

MO: Misuse of Resources

Impact: Disrupt

Target Sector: Com

3.7 Maroochy Water System (2000)

In Maroochy Shire, Queensland, Australia in 2000 a disgruntled ex-employee hacked into a water control system and flooded the grounds of a hotel and a nearby river with a million litres of sewage. The Maroochy Shire attack was not one attack but a whole series of attacks over a prolonged period [6].

Source Sector: Intl

MO: Misuse of Resources, User Compromise

Impact: Disrupt

Target Sector: Intl

3.8 California System Operator (2001)

Attackers, possibly from China, were able to gain access into one of the computer networks at the California Independent System Operator (Cal-ISO) in May 2001. The Cal-ISO has hierarchical control over a number of PCS networks operated by its constituent transmission owners. This hack was unsuccessful at penetrating any PCS network, yet it uncomfortably extended a period of longer than two weeks [9].

Source Sector: Intl

MO: Root Compromise

Impact: Unknown

Target Sector: Gov

3.9 Davis-Besse Nuclear Power Plant (2003)

In January 2003, the SQL Slammer worm infected the Davis Besse nuclear power plant in Ohio, USA. As a result of the worm's activity, the plant's Safety Parameter Display System and Plant Process Computer were disabled for several hours [8].

Source Sector: Unknown

MO: Worm

Impact: Disrupt

Target Sector: Com

3.10 CSX Corporation (2003)

In a similar case to the SQLSlammer worm, also in 2003, a computer virus named Sobig was reported to have shut down train signaling systems in Florida, U.S. The virus was reported to have been one of the fastest spreading e-mail attachment viruses at the time. It shut down the signaling, dispatching and other systems at CSX Corporation; one of the largest transportation suppliers in the U.S. While there were no major incidents caused by this case, trains were delayed [7].

Source Sector: Unknown

MO: Virus

Impact: Disrupt

Target Sector: Com

3.11 Tehama Colusa Canal Authority (2007)

A former electrical supervisor at Tehama Colusa Canal Authority (TCAA) installed unauthorized software on the TCAA's SCADA system. The employee is reported to have installed the software on the day that he was dismissed, having worked at the company for 17 years. No technical reports or analysis have been publicly released that detail the unauthorized software, nor has there been any insight as to whether or not damage was caused [7].

Source Sector: User

MO: Misuse of Resources

Impact: Unknown

Target Sector: Gov

3.12 Stuxnet (2010)

In June 2010, it was discovered that a worm dubbed Stuxnet had struck the Iranian nuclear facility at Natanz. Stuxnet used four 'zero-day vulnerabilities' (vulnerabilities previously unknown, so there has been no time to develop and distribute patches). The worm employs Siemens' default passwords to access Windows operating systems that run WinCC and PCS7 programs. The worm would hunt down frequency-converter drives made by Fararo Paya in Iran and Vacon in Finland. These drives were used to power centrifuges used in the concentration of the uranium-235 isotope. Stuxnet altered the frequency of the electrical current to the drives causing them to switch between high and low speeds for which they were not designed. This switching caused the centrifuges to fail at a higher than normal rate [4].

Source Sector: Intl

MO: Worm, Root Compromise, Trojan

Impact: Disrupt, Distort

Target Sector: Intl

3.13 Night Dragon (2011)

In February 2011 McAfee reported that five global energy and oil firms were targeted by a combination of attacks including social engineering, trojans and Windows-based exploits. The attacks, code-named 'Night Dragon', have been confirmed to have been ongoing for over two years and are believed to have been of Chinese origin. It is noted that the attackers may simply be using Chinese tools and compromised Chinese computers in order to mask their identity. While no SCADA systems were directly attacked, the corporate network segments belonging to companies that operate SCADA infrastructures were attacked. It is reported that attackers exfiltrated data such as operational blueprints [7].

Source Sector: Intl

MO: Social Engineering, User Compromise, Root Compromise

Impact: Disclosure

Target Sector: Intl

3.14 DUQU (2011)

In 2011, Virus Researchers discovered a new form of Malware that utilized many of the same techniques as Stuxnet. The new code was named Duqu and contained parts that were nearly identical to Stuxnet. Duqu was not self-replicating and did not contain a payload. It appears to be designed to conduct reconnaissance on an unknown industrial control system [13].

Source Sector: Intl

MO: Virus

Impact: Disclosure

Target Sector: Intl

3.15 Flame (2012)

Researchers have recently discovered a piece of malware operating in Iran, Lebanon, Syria, Sudan, the West Bank and other places in the Middle East and North Africa for at least two years. This malware dubbed "Flame" appears to be sponsored by the same group that was behind Stuxnet. Early analysis indicates that it's designed primarily to spy on the users of infected computers and steal data, including documents, recorded conversations and keystrokes. It also opens a backdoor to infected systems to allow the attackers to tweak the toolkit and add new functionality. Flame was discovered after the United Nations International Telecommunications Union asked researchers to look into reports in April that computers belonging to the Iranian Oil Ministry and the Iranian National Oil Co. had been hit with malware that was stealing and deleting information from the systems [12].

Source Sector: Unknown

MO: Worm

Impact: Disclosure, Destruct

Target Sector: Intl

Table 2: Summary of Incidents

Year	Title	Source Sector	MO	Impact	Target Sector
1982	Siberian Pipeline Explosion	Unknown	Trojan	Distort	Intl
1992	Chevron Emergency Alert System	User	Misuse of Resources, User Compromise	Disrupt	Com
1994	Salt River Project	User	Root Compromise, Trojan	Disclosure	Gov
1997	Worcester, MA Airport	User	Root Compromise, Denial of Service	Disrupt	Gov
1999	Gazprom	Intl	User Compromise, Trojan	Disrupt	Intl
1999	Bellingham, WA Gas Pipeline	User	Misuse of Resources	Disrupt	Com
2000	Maroochy Water System	Intl	Misuse of Resources, User Compromise	Disrupt	Intl
2001	California Systems Operator	Intl	Root Compromise	Unknown	Gov
2003	Davis-Besse Nuclear Power Plant	Unknown	Worm	Disrupt	Com
2003	CSX Corporation	Unknown	Virus	Disrupt	Com
2007	Tehama Colusa Canal Authority	User	Misuse of Resources	Unknown	Gov
2010	Stuxnet	Intl	Worm, Root Compromise, Trojan	Disrupt, Distort	Intl
2011	Night Dragon	Intl	Social Engineering, User Compromise, Root Compromise	Disclosure	Intl
2011	Duqu	Intl	Virus	Disclosure	Intl
2012	Flame	Unknown	Worm	Disclosure, Destruct	Intl

4. ANALYSIS OF INCIDENTS

Figure 1 represents the Source Sectors for the attacks surveyed in Section 3. We found five attacks from International sources, four were a single user source and four were unknown.

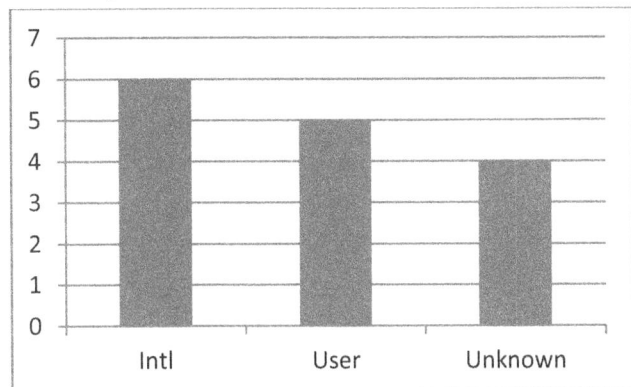

Figure 1: Source Sectors

Figure 2 details the attacks by Method of Operations. Five of the attacks surveyed utilized a Root Compromise, four took advantage of a User Compromise, four others used a Trojan, three of the attacks involved a Misuse of Resources, two attacks used a Worm, one utilized a Denial of Service, one was a Virus, and one was a Social Engineering attack.

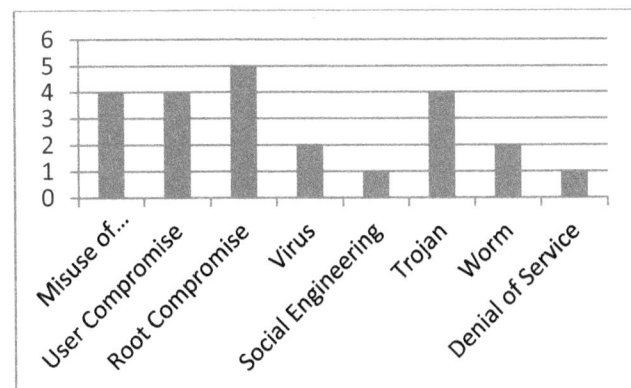

Figure 2: Method of Operations

We next look at the Impact of these attacks. The majority of the attacks disrupted operations, three disclosed data, two distorted data, one destroyed data, and one had unknown impact.

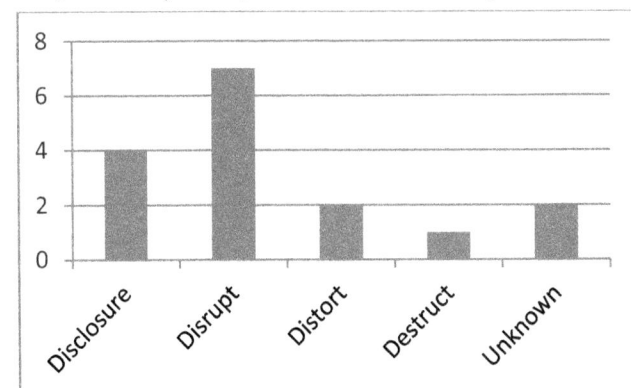

Figure 3: Impact

The Target Sectors of the attacks break down as follows. Five attacks were against Intl targets, four were Gov, and 3 were Com.

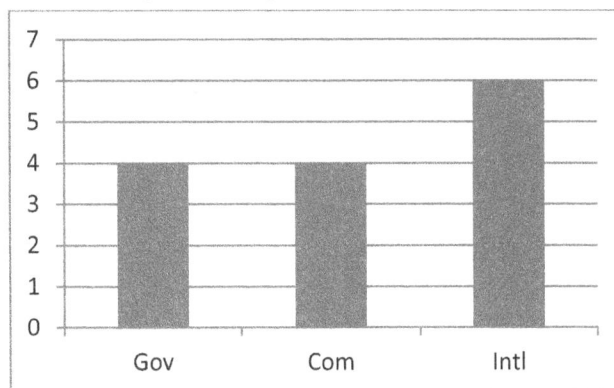

Figure 4: Target Sectors

The frequency of incidents is increasing as can be seen when we chart the number of incidents by year.

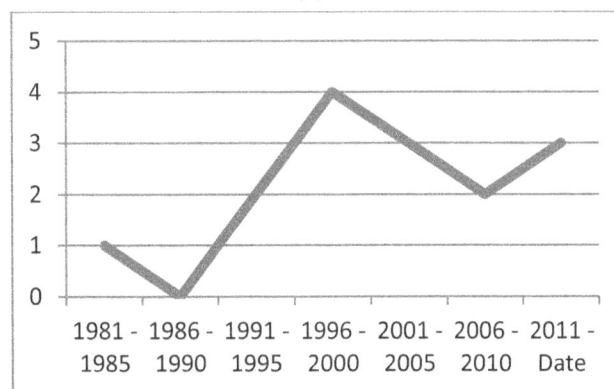

Figure 5: Incidents by Year

Care should be taken in interpreting these above figures due to the incomplete dataset. The incidents covered represent some of the more visible and documented attacks to date but is incomplete. In the creation of a database to analyze such attacks we intend to provide a quantifiable measure for identifying and subsequently presenting 'significant' attacks.

5. CONCLUSIONS

The preceding list and analysis is a sampling of malware attacks. To include a complete list would extend this paper well beyond its intended length. As of 2005, the RISI database included over 120 such incidents [11]. Understanding the nature of SCADA attacks and their evolution over time can assist the development of new techniques to mitigate their impact. We propose compiling a comprehensive database of incidents using a standardized terminology and quantifiable data to determine the severity of the incident. We also propose making such information freely available to other academic and nonprofit research organizations. This database shall include references to research papers that present an interpretation of an incident.

6. ACKNOWLEDGEMENTS

We acknowledge and thank the individuals and organizations that have taken significant steps in documenting SCADA incidents.

7. REFERENCES

[1] Cheung, S. et al. 2006. Using Model-based Intrusion Detection for SCADA Networks.

[2] Daniela, T. 2011. Communication security in SCADA pipeline monitoring systems. *Roedunet International Conference (RoEduNet), 2011 10th*.

[3] Denning, D.E. 2000. Cyberterrorism: The Logic Bomb versus the Truck Bomb - Centre for World Dialogue. *Global Dialogue*. 2, 4 (2000).

[4] Farwell, J.P. and Rohozinski, R. 2011. Stuxnet and the Future of Cyber War. *Survival*. 53, 1 (Feb. 2011), 23–40.

[5] Kjaerland, M. 2006. A taxonomy and comparison of computer security incidents from the commercial and government sectors. *Computers & Security*. 25, 7 (Oct. 2006), 522–538.

[6] Mustard, S. 2005. Security of distributed control systems: the concern increases. *Computing & Control Engineering Journal*.

[7] Nicholson, A. et al. 2012. SCADA Security in the light of Cyber-Warfare. *Computers & Security*. 31, 4 (Mar. 2012), 436–418.

[8] Remenyi, E. by D.D. et al. 2006. *Proceedings of the 5th European Conference on Information Warfare and Security: National Defence College, Helsinki, Finland, 1 - 2 June 2006*. Academic Conferences Limited.

[9] Stamp, J. et al. 2003. Common vulnerabilities in critical infrastructure control systems. *Sandia National Laboratories*. (2003).

[10] Tsang, R. Cyberthreats, Vulnerabilities and Attacks on SCADA Networks.

[11] Turk, R.J. 2005. Cyber Incidents Involving Control Systems. *Contract*. October (2005).

[12] Zetter, K. 2012. "Flame" spyware infiltrating Iranian computers - CNN.com. *Wired*.

[13] Zetter, K. 2011. Son of Stuxnet Found in the Wild on Systems in Europe. *Wired*.

Improving Accuracy in Face Tracking
User Interfaces using Consumer Devices

Norman H. Villaroman
Brigham Young University
Information Technology Program
Provo, Utah
normanhv@byu.edu

Dale C. Rowe Ph.D.
Brigham Young University
Information Technology Program
Provo, Utah
+1 (801) 422 6051
dale_rowe@byu.edu

ABSTRACT
Using face and head movements to control a computer can be especially helpful for users who, for various reasons, cannot effectively use common input devices with their hands. Using vision-based consumer devices makes such a user interface readily available and allows its use to be non-intrusive. However, a characteristic problem with this system is accurate control. Consumer devices capture already small face movements at a resolution that is usually lower than the screen resolution. Computer vision algorithms and technologies that enable such also introduce noise, adversely affecting usability. This paper describes how different components of this perceptual user interface contribute to the problem of accuracy and presents potential solutions. This interface was implemented with different configurations and was statistically evaluated to support the analysis. The different configurations include, among other things, the use of 2D and depth images from consumer devices, different input styles, and the use of the Kalman filter.

Categories and Subject Descriptors
H.5.2 [**Information Interfaces and Presentation**]: User Interfaces – *Input devices and strategies.*

K.4.2 [**Computers and Society**]: Social Issues – *Assistive technologies for persons with disabilities.*

I.4.8 [**Image Processing and Computer Vision**]: Scene Analysis – *Object recognition, Tracking.*

I.5.5 [**Image Processing and Computer Vision**]: Implementation – *Interactive systems.*

General Terms
Design, Human Factors

Keywords
Face, Detection, Tracking, Accessibility, Depth, Perceptual User Interface, Consumer Devices, Assistive Technology

1. INTRODUCTION
Users with certain disabilities may find it very difficult, if not totally impossible, to use standard input devices such as the

ubiquitous mouse and keyboard. The user interface described in this paper is one in which users can provide cursor and selection control to a computer just by using natural head and face movements captured by vision-based devices to make it non-intrusive. This perceptual user interface covers several topics in Information Technology including accessibility, interface design, and algorithms, to name a few.[14] This work considers various options in designing a face tracking perceptual user interface and evaluates their implications for accurate control. Some solutions are discussed and some prototypes were implemented and were statistically evaluated to support the analysis.

2. RELATED WORK
Face tracking user interfaces using consumer devices are not new. [11] The application *SINA* of Varona et al. detected and tracked the nose from image features for cursor control and eye winks from color distributions for control commands.[23] The earlier application *Nouse* of Gorodnichy et al. tracked the nose and eyes as well and used multiple blinks as control commands. [9] They also proposed and implemented a visual feedback mechanism where a small image follows the cursor and shows how the system is interpreting the current state of the user's face pose.[7] Morris et al. used skin color to detect the face and the nostrils, producing a system that they admit is vulnerable to noise from similarly colored regions.[17] Chathuranga et al. implemented a system where the nose is tracked for cursor control and where speech recognition is used for selection.[4] The *Camera Mouse* uses correlation to track user-defined and automatically updating templates to track a small region in a video sequence.[2] Muchun et al. detected eye blinks using pattern matching and optical flow.[18] Other eye tracking user interfaces have also been studied and developed. [10,20]

While this research has the same intended application as some of these mentioned works, it is different in the design and implementation options presented in that more such options are now available. These differences are brought about by, among other things, advancement of technology and algorithms.

Many perceptual user interfaces primarily use image streams from a regular camera. Recent advances in sensor technology have added a new dimension, literally and figuratively, to vision-based applications that are readily available to consumers. The launch of the *Microsoft Kinect* in November 2010 spurred the development of a wide variety of commercial applications and research work. While various depth sensors have been used before, the *Kinect* made a relatively high resolution (640x480) depth sensor available at a very low price. Some relevant works include those which use its depth data to detect and track face pose [6,13] and to create 3D face models. [26]

3. FACING THE ACCURACY PROBLEM

The primary problem of face tracking user interfaces is accuracy. This is a common issue for all natural user interaction systems. However, the problem is exacerbated in a face tracking scenario due to the small window of facial movement and the need to control a cursor in higher resolution screens. The problem is further compounded by the development of high resolution displays.

To better illustrate this problem, we estimated the span of normal face movement (without moving the torso and still is in convenient view of the screen) of a user about 24 inches from a screen and a 640x480 imaging sensor. We found that normal yaw and pitch movements of this user's face while still having a more or less convenient view of the screen only covers about 100x100 pixels in the field of view or about 84° for either rotation. This small region presents obvious challenges when trying to control, say, a 1920x1080 screen.

We discuss accuracy considerations according to the logical components of the input data flow, which we define as follows.

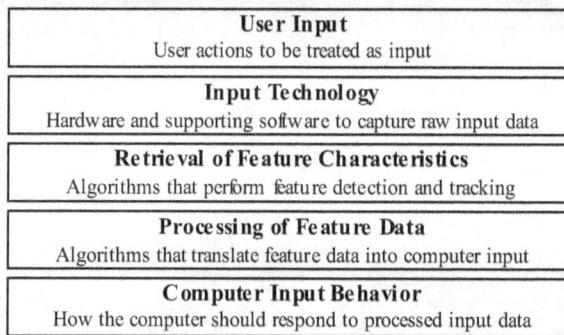

User Input
User actions to be treated as input
Input Technology
Hardware and supporting software to capture raw input data
Retrieval of Feature Characteristics
Algorithms that perform feature detection and tracking
Processing of Feature Data
Algorithms that translate feature data into computer input
Computer Input Behavior
How the computer should respond to processed input data

Figure 1. Input components by data flow

It should be noted that we acknowledge the presence of several other issues and considerations in this user interface. In particular, the question of usability would undoubtedly be a primary factor in the design decisions. However, at this stage, our research is focused on the technical feasibility of creating robust solutions that may be used in usability testing. It is important for these solutions to be robust because with a naturally learned interface, erratic responses can easily make it unacceptable. For the time being, we defer usability studies to follow-on research and focus on how these different components affect accuracy.

3.1 User Input

A primary consideration for any user interface is what the user does that would be interpreted as input. This affects the accuracy requirement on the feature processing component.

3.1.1 Cursor Control

For cursor control, the options that were considered for how a user's face movement is interpreted include:

- 3D Location and Pose - uses the 3D location of the face and the direction of the face pose

- 2D Location - uses only the 2D location of the face

Another set of options determine how a physical interaction zone [15] is defined. This defines the limits of the interface and should be a subset of the user's physical limits. Options that were considered for this include:

- Absolute - the representation of this zone in the real-world is fixed and may span the entire field-of-view

- Relative - the representation of this zone in the real-world moves with the user (e.g. drawn from a rectangular area above the user's shoulders)

The combinations of these options can be and should be reviewed in a usability study. However, for evaluating accuracy, what really matters in defining the interaction zone is not whether the zone is fixed or not but what the size of the zone is. The combinations of options considered for this paper are:

- 3D location and pose with an absolute interaction zone that spans the entire field-of-view. Note that this kind of interaction zone is only possible because the 3D location and pose are used.

- 2D location with an interaction zone that only spans the limits of comfortable face movement with a fixed torso.

The first would be ideal and would provide greater flexibility if it can be implemented robustly enough. It makes the face an absolute pointing mechanism that is robust to variance in the user's physical location in the workstation area. However, using face pose would generally require a greater degree of accuracy primarily because it requires a larger set of features to be analyzed (e.g. two 3D points that determine the pose vector, or a plane and its normal through a point, etc.) whereas only one 2D point is needed for face location. An absolute pointing user input also reduces the effective limits of the face pose to the actual screen area which otherwise could be extended as long as the eyes can still comfortably gaze at the screen. On the other hand, the additional features provided by 3D face pose can mitigate the resolution problem if its calculation is extremely accurate.

The second is a simpler option and requires less of vision processing than the first. It is the same cursor control method that *Camera Mouse* implements. [2] Though this is simpler, this poses a burden on usability. For one, because face pose is not available by definition, the interaction zone has to be limited to a small region covering normal face movements. It will improve usability if the definition of this region happens automatically and adjusts to the user's varying positions (e.g. leaning in any direction). This can be done by detection of the shoulders, the calculation of the head's centroid, and/or using depth information of the feature. Manual calibration techniques to define this region have been implemented in previous works. *Nouse* implements a fixed interaction zone within the field of view that can be re-initialized (i.e. the process is still not fully automatic).[9] *Camera Mouse* requires the user or a helper to specify the reference point and sensitivity (interaction zone size) by a mouse click.[2] We believe that a fully automatic definition of the interaction zone will improve usability significantly.

Another issue on the use of just the location in cursor control is that the normal movements of the face (without the torso moving) are generally comprised of rotations and not translations. So the location would have to be calculated from face yaw and pitch rotations. And the variation in the image characteristics (e.g. shadows) that the rotations produce can make vision processing more challenging.

3.1.2 Selection Control and Other Commands

While cursor control by itself can provide selection based on dwell time, having other options available for selection would cater to the preference of a wider user base. Examples of facial gestures for selection or other special commands include opening the mouth, sticking out the tongue, raising eyebrows, and prolonged or multiple blinks, among others. As with other natural user interfaces, the *Midas touch* problem, where the user accidentally triggers commands from natural movement, has to be mitigated sufficiently. This requires accurate retrieval and processing of feature characteristics (see Section 3.3). It would also be helpful to program a gesture to turn the cursor or selection control on and off similar to the Snap Clutch of Istance et al.[12] and other face tracking user interfaces. [9,23]

3.2 Input Technology

Various devices can enable the input on a face tracking user interface. While there are potentially many such, we only discuss two classes of vision-based consumer devices for input because they are non-intrusive and are readily available to users.

3.2.1 2D Image Cameras

A regular camera is utilized in many vision-based applications and much research has been done that deal with its 2D images. In favor of this input technology is its ability for high resolution capture and its ubiquity. While object location and boundaries are consistent (as opposed to, for example, noisy depth images from some consumer sensors), noise is introduced by illumination changes and by the presence of other objects in the field-of-view that can break the characteristics of relevant objects due to occlusion or camouflaging, among other things.

3.2.2 Consumer Depth Sensors

It has been noted that consumer depth sensors have recently gained popularity and outcomes that have been accomplished or are being worked on are done with the additional depth data available. Such sensors include the *Microsoft Kinect* and the *Asus Xtion* and are based on light coding technology developed by PrimeSense where depth calculations are done in parallel from reflection of structured infrared light.[21] While it is great for seeing small indoor scenes in 3D, we have found that noise in its depth measurements make fine depth variation hard to detect. The edges of objects in the depth image have noise that makes the edges unreliable for precise calculations. In addition, surfaces that exhibit high specular reflection as well as external sources of IR light (e.g. sunlight) can produce erroneous depth readings.

Although the depth image from such sensors is noisier pixel-wise than its color/grayscale counterpart, it provides additional data that can be very helpful. For one, it is able to provide true depth more accurately and easily compared to other monocular consumer image sensors. It solves the relatively hard problem of correspondence search in stereo reconstruction from natural light. Segmentation of the foreground also becomes a simpler task. It is also able to keep track of objects in its practical field-of-view in ambient or varying lighting conditions.

These sensors will usually have a built in RGB camera so the image and the depth data can be registered and used together. Various libraries can be used to capture and process data from these sensors. These include *OpenNI*, the *Point Cloud Library*, and the *Microsoft Kinect for Windows SDK*.

3.3 Retrieval of Feature Characteristics

Feature characteristics can be collected using various detection and other vision processing algorithms. This is a widely researched topic in computer vision and in no way does this paper attempt to give a comprehensive discussion on it. It is mentioned here for completeness as well as to give a high-level overview of noise considerations in the selection and use of such algorithms. We feel that this component is of utmost importance and requires a high degree of robustness. Anything short of this can easily make a poor user interface.

One critical question is that of determining which feature or features to use for the interface. The answer depends on the input technology used as discussed in the previous section and how that feature can be robustly detected and tracked. The nose has been recommended as a good feature to track from regular images in this scenario because of its visibility and consistent intensity profile in various poses.[8] Regular images also provide characteristically high intensity gradients for the eyes. However, in a noisy depth image, the eye on its own is harder to differentiate from another relatively flat patch. In a depth image the nose is more prominent. Weise et al. used the entire face excluding the jaw area for rigid tracking from depth images.[26] The feature or a combination of such features to be detected has to be unique in the image and removal of non-relevant data by segmentation or otherwise would be helpful in making this happen. Using a combination of features can provide a confidence level that can be adjusted to reduce false positives. In addition, algorithms should also process at the sub-pixel level (e.g. using the data type *float* for point coordinates instead of *int*) whenever possible and appropriate.

In the following sections, we particularly mention surveys of computer vision methods as they can be very helpful in understanding the level of accuracy these methods can come with. It should be kept in mind that this user interface operates in a constrained environment where the background does not really move, the imaging device is stationary, and the user is the primary foreground object. Occlusions other than the possibility of glasses and rotation will be uncommon and unexpected. Pre-processing methods like background subtraction by image differencing or depth segmentation are definitely helpful.

Various open-source and commercial libraries already have implementations of the detection, tracking, and pose estimation algorithms mentioned here. These include, among others, the work of Fanelli et al.,[6] *Point Cloud Library*, *OpenCV*, *Seeing Machines' faceAPI*,[22] and the *Microsoft Face Tracking SDK*. We have investigated the capabilities of these libraries for face detection but, due to space limitations, only a couple of them are included as implementation options presented here.

3.3.1 Feature Detection

Zhang and Zhang published a survey on face detection in 2010 [30] to update a similar survey by Ming-Hsuan et al.[16] The survey on object tracking by Yilmaz et al. also contains a general survey on object detection which can help in the selection of which feature to detect.[28] These surveys can help in the selection and implementation of these algorithms.

The object detection framework of Viola and Jones [24] was a landmark work that made face detection more practical in real-time applications for its speed and effectiveness.[30] To provide an example, we evaluate the suitability of the Viola-Jones detector in a face tracking user interface, at the same time acknowledging that much has been done since to improve face detection and that this is not meant to be a review of all possible methods. Note that other face detectors we have seen exhibit some of the same characteristics that are good to consider in the algorithm selection.

It is able to detect faces (or other facial features) in real-time and on a per-frame basis with the use of highly efficient integral images and cascade classifiers. Particularly when detection per frame is counted, it yields some false positives and negatives which can easily break the usability of a face tracking user interface when used in one. Variability of the boundary of the detection frame also introduces noise in representing the face location. In addition, it is not robust to face rotation. All of these make it insufficient on its own to enable this user interface.

Depth data can help simplify the detection problem by providing additional recognizable data. For example, false positives will be reduced if the depth data can confirm that the detected feature is not on a head. A 3D head can also be detected first then image processing can help detect and fix the location of additional features. In other words, for robustness, we recommend the use of multiple detection methods where one makes up for the weaknesses of the others. These methods should also be robust to at least a small degree of rotation invariance.

While the ability to detect per frame shows the computational efficiency of an algorithm, we believe that this, in general, introduces noise and ignores valuable *a priori* knowledge. We believe that, to a certain degree, robust detection even with slightly longer computation time (coupled with real-time tracking) is more advantageous than a faster but less robust alternative.

3.3.2 Tracking

For most users, face movement will be generally smooth and tracking can help realize this. Yilmaz et al. did a survey on tracking methods in 2006.[28] It divided object tracking into point, kernel and silhouette tracking. Point tracking methods find corresponding points in subsequent frames and would usually be appropriate for tracking smaller objects. This may be appropriate if small features are tracked such as the eyes or nose. Kernel tracking methods use the object's shape and appearance and a motion vector is produced from parametric transformation of the object. This may be more appropriate for tracking the head or face. Silhouette tracking can be useful for certain face gesture detection. This survey referred to works that used regular 2D images. Some of them may be applicable to 3D point clouds. However, if depth images from consumer depth sensors are used, the noise in the object boundaries will cause inaccuracy in the results so the use of such boundaries should be avoided.

3.3.3 Pose Estimation

If face pose estimation is accurate enough, it can prove to be very useful in processing input. Murphy-Chutorian and Trivedi presented an excellent comprehensive survey of such methods with an annotated comparison of accuracy in 2009 with a separate evaluation for fine and coarse estimation. [19] Some of the fine estimation methods in these works show promise. [25,29] However, as they noted, many of the works reviewed make assumptions or use methods that make them less applicable in real-world and real-time applications. These include limitation to a single rotational degree-of-freedom, requirement of manual intervention, familiar identity (i.e. where the test data is very similar to the training data), and requirement of specialized setups or non-consumer sensors, among others. They have identified these assumptions and associated them whenever applicable with the reviewed methods. While these methods had been or could be improved by more recent technology, techniques, or datasets, we recommend the use of this survey in the selection of face pose estimation methods particularly because of the comparison on accuracy.

Recent works on face pose estimation using depth information address some of these limitations and, perhaps with some improvement or modification, are appropriate in real-world face tracking user interfaces.[1,5,13,26]

Tracking methods may also be applicable and useful here to capture smooth movement and some pose estimation methods

already use them.[19] A method worth noting for its potential to track face location and pose accurately using 3D point clouds is Iterative Closest Point (ICP) as used by Weise et al. [26]

3.4 Processing of Feature Data

Because the collected feature data is expected to have noise, it is essential to process it into data that is more appropriate as input. A cursor that jumps around and on and off the target will not be usable. A number of algorithms can be used to mitigate this noise on the calculated cursor point. The tracking problem in this case is much simpler than traditional object tracking in video sequences. Calculated cursor points come in sequence and the goal of the algorithm is to yield points that are smooth and are more representative of the user's actual face movement.

While other methods could be used such as mean/median filters, mean-shift,[23] or particle filters, we show that the Kalman filter is an appropriate method to use in this scenario, contrary to a previous finding.[23] The classic Kalman filter can operate on a simple time-discrete linear model such as this one and is relatively resilient to outliers and noise in general. As a recursive Bayesian method, it provides an efficient way of estimating the true state of an object by recursively predicting the next state and updating it with new observations if there are any. It asks for parameters for the process model, control input (which is not necessarily applicable in this case), new measurements or observations, and noise in the process and in the observations. A simple way of applying this filter to the stream of noisy cursor input data include 1) having the position and the velocity in both axes of the cursor define the state, 2) modeling the point location as a function of previous location and velocity, 3) using the new cursor points from the feature data as measurements, and 4) making sure that the real noise distribution is not too far from Gaussian white noise assumed by the filter. Similar techniques are helpful not only in the final calculated cursor point but in other data sets along the process flow as well (e.g. face pose vector, etc.).

3.5 Computer Input Behavior

Computer input behavior determines how the cursor moves given the final calculation of feature data. The two options investigated for cursor control include:

- Location - the calculated date vector will be translated into a point on the screen.
- Velocity - the calculated data vector will determine the direction and the velocity of the cursor movement relative to its previous position.

The first requires more accuracy because it scales with the screen resolution whereas the second does not. Previous works have implemented and recommended the second because of this less stringent accuracy requirement. [9,23] This makes the face work like a joystick, which may not be very ideal because a joystick goes back to its center position on its own while the face does not. Improvements in technology and computer vision techniques allow us to consider and use the first, which can prove to be more usable, as a viable option.

4. IMPLEMENTATION

Basic face tracking user interfaces were implemented that used some of the options discussed in this paper. The goal of this is to understand the challenges on accuracy of the different input components, thereby getting better insights to their solutions, and to validate the analysis done. While we are not presenting all the options we implemented due to space limitation, we also did not exhaustively implement and test all the possible options and their combinations as we feel they are not necessary for the purposes of this paper.

We are not so concerned about ground truth of the face location or pose as long as the cursor responds to general face movements and the user's eyes are still able to comfortably get visual feedback of how the cursor is responding. For this paper, we are concerned with the ability to accurately target a specific region and so we analyzed the spread of the generated cursor points and how they are affected by various input components.

4.1 Experimental Setup
Development was done on a Windows 7 machine with an Intel® Core™ i5-2500 (3.3 GHz) CPU and 8GB of memory. The applications were written in Visual C++. A web camera (in 640x480 mode) was used and a Microsoft Kinect sensor.

For every combination of input options a subject was asked to look directly at a 23-in 1920x1080 screen and be still. Although, it is possible for noise to be present at different angles of the face pose, we exclude those options in this paper for brevity. We only used five seconds of data which was programmatically timed. Our basis for this is that this time is generally sufficient to aim a cursor using conventional hand-held methods. We retrieved the stream of calculated pair-wise points, which then translates to screen pixels.

4.2 User Input
The cursor control options were implemented as enumerated and described in Section 3.1.1. The option that uses the 2D location of a feature point with a physical interaction zone defined by the limits of comfortable neck and face movements is called "2D Location" in the results. The one that uses 3D face pose and location in an absolute pointing mechanism is called "Absolute Pointing"

4.3 Input Technology and Feature Retrieval
We used two existing face/head detection and tracking implementations - one from a regular camera and the other from pure depth generated by a Kinect sensor. It is not intended to compare the two implementations against each other as the comparison would not be on level ground. The purpose of using these implementations is to show how a face tracking user interface can be enabled by the two classes of input technology mentioned. They were chosen because they were found to be sufficiently robust to scale and rotation, they do face detection, tracking and pose estimation automatically, and they have available code or API that expose the face location and pose.

4.3.1 Using 2D Images
Seeing Machine's faceAPI [22] was used as the face tracking engine of this implementation. It is a commercial and proprietary product. As such, we cannot comment on how it accomplishes face tracking but that it does it very well. Among other things, it provides the location of the detected face and its orientation in radians, which is sufficient for the purpose of the user interface in study. True depth was provided manually as 24 inches where necessary as an estimate of the user's distance from the screen/sensor. This is called "2D" in the results.

4.3.2 Using Depth Images
The face detection and pose estimation engine used for this implementation is the work done by Fanelli et al specifically with consumer depth sensors. [5,6] They used forests of randomly trained decision trees [3] for both classification (head detection) and regression (pose estimation) using solely the depth data. It recalculates per frame and runs in real-time on a state-of-the-art desktop. The head pose in each frame of the sequence was determined using ICP with a personalized template constructed using an online model building approach by Weise et al.[26,27]

We used the default stride value of 5, which determines the balance between accuracy and speed. We discovered that speed is adversely affected by the inclusion of larger depth patches (e.g. user's body) and a shorter distance to the sensor, presumably because the training data had subjects at 1m away. In consequence, we had the subject sit from 1m away for a more real-time response. It was not expected that the pose estimation here will be accurate as published best results indicate a yaw error of $8.9\pm13.0°$.[5,6] This is called "Depth" in the results.

4.4 Processing of Feature Data
The Kalman filter implementation in OpenCV 2.3 was used according to the suggestions made in Section 3.4. The standard deviation of the calculated points without the Kalman filter was used to model the noise covariance matrices of the filter.

5. RESULTS
The results obtained are expected and they validate the analysis, of which the following table is a partial summary.

Table 1. Standard deviation in the horizontal and vertical axes (rounded to the nearest integer)

	2D Location		Absolute Pointing	
	--	Kalman	--	Kalman
Depth	29, 20	21, 14	59, 16	14, 11
2D	14, 5	9, 2	18, 13	7, 10

The results show that the Kalman filter improved the accuracy of the cursor points in all cases and more so in options that have more noise without it. Using 2D location was also generally more accurate except arguably with the depth method. This can be explained by the fact that the location was derived from the face pose vector which is the design and purpose of the algorithm (as opposed to getting the 2D location of a point directly). The best combination allows the user to control the cursor sufficiently well which is confirmed by its minimal variance.

It has to be noted that we separated the results for the horizontal and vertical axes to show that face tracking algorithms can respond differently on both axes and may have different noise models, which is confirmed by our data. The detection and tracking algorithms play a significant role in this difference. Understanding this helps in using more accurate noise models and in the selection and implementation of vision algorithms.

6. CONCLUSION
We have enumerated the different input components of a face tracking user interface and discussed considerations for each on improving accuracy. These components were implemented with some of the options discussed. Similar to the suggestion given by Fanelli et al, [5] we confirm the benefit of using both image and depth data, especially when a consumer device that can provide both is readily available (e.g. *Kinect*). The implementations served to validate the understanding and the analysis of the challenges on making face tracking user interfaces more accurate, which would then serve as a stepping stone to usability studies. A statistical analysis was also made that provided additional insights on some useful methods that can be used in the design of such interfaces.

7. REFERENCES

[1] ALDOMA, A. *Progress on head detection and pose estimation (II).* http://pointclouds.org/blog/hrcs/ (Last Accessed: July 2012)

[2] BETKE, M., GIPS, J., et al., 2002. The Camera Mouse: visual tracking of body features to provide computer access for people with severe disabilities. *Neural Systems and Rehabilitation Engineering, IEEE Transactions on 10*, 1, 1-10.

[3] BREIMAN, L., 2001. Random Forests. *Mach. Learn. 45*, 1, 5-32. DOI= http://dx.doi.org/10.1023/a:1010933404324.

[4] CHATHURANGA, S.K., SAMARAWICKRAMA, K.C., et al., 2010. Hands free interface for Human Computer Interaction. In *Information and Automation for Sustainability (ICIAFs), 2010 5th International Conference on*, 359-364.

[5] FANELLI, G., GALL, J., et al., 2012. Real Time 3D Head Pose Estimation: Recent Achievements and Future Challenges. In *Communications, Control and Signal Processing, 2012. ISCCSP 2012. 5th International Symposium on*.

[6] FANELLI, G., WEISE, T., et al., 2011. Real Time Head Pose Estimation from Consumer Depth Cameras. In *DAGM'11*, Frankfurt, Germany.

[7] GORODNICHY, D., 2006. *Perceptual Cursor - A Solution to the Broken Loop Problem in Vision-Based Hands-Free Computer Control Devices.*

[8] GORODNICHY, D.O., 2002. On importance of nose for face tracking. In *Automatic Face and Gesture Recognition, 2002. Proceedings. Fifth IEEE International Conference on*, 181-186. DOI= http://dx.doi.org/10.1109/afgr.2002.1004153.

[9] GORODNICHY, D.O. and ROTH, G., 2004. Nouse 'use your nose as a mouse' perceptual vision technology for hands-free games and interfaces. *Image and Vision Computing 22*, 12, 931-942. DOI= http://dx.doi.org/10.1016/j.imavis.2004.03.021.

[10] HEIKKIL, H., #228, et al., 2012. Simple gaze gestures and the closure of the eyes as an interaction technique. In *Proceedings of the Proceedings of the Symposium on Eye Tracking Research and Applications* (Santa Barbara, California2012), ACM, 2168579, 147-154. DOI= http://dx.doi.org/10.1145/2168556.2168579.

[11] HUNKE, M. and WAIBEL, A., 1994. Face locating and tracking for human-computer interaction. In *Signals, Systems and Computers, 1994. 1994 Conference Record of the Twenty-Eighth Asilomar Conference on*, 1277-1281 vol.1272. DOI= http://dx.doi.org/10.1109/acssc.1994.471664.

[12] ISTANCE, H., BATES, R., et al., 2008. Snap Clutch, a Moded Approach to Solving the Midas Touch Problem. In *Proceedings of the Eye Tracking Research and Applications Symposium 2008* ACM, 221-228. DOI= http://dx.doi.org/citeulike-article-id:2603228.

[13] KONDORI, F.A., YOUSEFI, S., et al., 2011. 3D head pose estimation using the Kinect. In *Wireless Communications and Signal Processing (WCSP), 2011 International Conference on*, 1-4. DOI= http://dx.doi.org/10.1109/wcsp.2011.6096866.

[14] LUNT, B., EKSTROM, J., et al. IT 2008. *Communications of the ACM 53*, 12, 133.

[15] MICROSOFT *Kinect for Windows Human Interface Guidelines v1.5.0.* 2012. http://www.microsoft.com/en-us/kinectforwindows/develop/learn.aspx (Last Accessed: May 2012)

[16] MING-HSUAN, Y., KRIEGMAN, D.J., et al., 2002. Detecting faces in images: a survey. *Pattern Analysis and Machine Intelligence, IEEE Transactions on 24*, 1, 34-58. DOI= http://dx.doi.org/10.1109/34.982883.

[17] MORRIS, T. and CHAUHAN, V., 2006. Facial feature tracking for cursor control. *Journal of Network and Computer Applications 29*, 1, 62-80. DOI= http://dx.doi.org/10.1016/j.jnca.2004.07.003.

[18] MUCHUN, S., CHINYEN, Y., et al., 2008. An implementation of an eye-blink-based communication aid for people with severe disabilities. In *Audio, Language and Image Processing, 2008. ICALIP 2008. International Conference on*, 351-356.

[19] MURPHY-CHUTORIAN, E. and TRIVEDI, M.M., 2009. Head Pose Estimation in Computer Vision: A Survey. *Pattern Analysis and Machine Intelligence, IEEE Transactions on 31*, 4, 607-626. DOI= http://dx.doi.org/10.1109/tpami.2008.106.

[20] PORTA, M. and TURINA, M., 2008. Eye-S: a full-screen input modality for pure eye-based communication. In *Proceedings of the Proceedings of the 2008 Symposium on Eye Tracking Research and Applications* (Savannah, Georgia2008), ACM, 1344477, 27-34. DOI= http://dx.doi.org/10.1145/1344471.1344477.

[21] PRIMESENSE *The PrimeSense 3D Awareness Sensor.* PrimeSense Ltd, http://primesense.com/press-room/resources/file/4-primesense-3d-sensor-data-sheet?lang=en (Last Accessed: May 2012)

[22] SEEING MACHINES *faceAPI.* http://www.seeingmachines.com/product/faceapi/ (Last Accessed: May 2012)

[23] VARONA, J., MANRESA-YEE, C., et al., 2008. Hands-free vision-based interface for computer accessibility. *Journal of Network and Computer Applications 31*, 4, 357-374. DOI= http://dx.doi.org/10.1016/j.jnca.2008.03.003.

[24] VIOLA, P. and JONES, M., 2001. Rapid object detection using a boosted cascade of simple features. In *Computer Vision and Pattern Recognition, 2001. CVPR 2001. Proceedings of the 2001 IEEE Computer Society Conference on*, I-511-I-518 vol.511.

[25] WANG, J.-G. and SUNG, E., 2007. EM enhancement of 3D head pose estimated by point at infinity. *Image and Vision Computing 25*, 12, 1864-1874. DOI= http://dx.doi.org/10.1016/j.imavis.2005.12.017.

[26] WEISE, T., BOUAZIZ, S., et al., 2011. Realtime performance-based facial animation. *ACM Trans. Graph. 30*, 4, 1-10. DOI= http://dx.doi.org/10.1145/2010324.1964972.

[27] WEISE, T., WISMER, T., et al., 2009. In-hand scanning with online loop closure. In *Computer Vision Workshops (ICCV Workshops), 2009 IEEE 12th International Conference on*, 1630-1637. DOI= http://dx.doi.org/10.1109/iccvw.2009.5457479.

[28] YILMAZ, A., JAVED, O., et al., 2006. Object tracking: A survey. *ACM Comput. Surv. 38*, 4, 13. DOI= http://dx.doi.org/10.1145/1177352.1177355.

[29] YUN, F. and HUANG, T.S., 2006. Graph embedded analysis for head pose estimation. In *Automatic Face and Gesture Recognition, 2006. FGR 2006. 7th International Conference on*, 6 pp.-8. DOI= http://dx.doi.org/10.1109/fgr.2006.60.

[30] ZHANG, C. and ZHANG, Z. *A Survey of Recent Advances in Face Detection.* Microsoft Research, 2010. http://research.microsoft.com/apps/pubs/default.aspx?id=132077 (Last Accessed: June 2012)

Author Index

Agresti, William W. 49

Brewer, Jeffrey L. 13

Bunton, Thomas E. 13

Ejnioui, Abdel 37

Ekstrom, Joseph J. 49

Friedman, Rob 49

Hacker, Thomas 43

Hansen, Andrew 19

Jasani, Hetal 1

Lunt, Barry M. 7, 19

Miller, Bill 51

Neupane, Bikalpa 19

Ofori, Richard 19

Otero, Carlos E. 37

Otero, Luis D. 37

Parks, Nancy E. 31

Reichgelt, Han 49

Robison, Nicholas 43

Rowe, Dale C. 7, 51, 57

Simco, Greg 25

Stockman, Mark 49

Villaroman, Norman H. 57

Yoas, Daniel W. 25

Resource Utilization Prediction:
A Proposal for Information Technology Research

Daniel W. Yoas
Nova Southeastern University
Pennsylvania College of Technology
Williamsport, PA 17701
yoas@nova.edu; dyoas@pct.edu

Greg Simco
Graduate School of Computer and Information Sciences
Nova Southeastern University
Ft. Lauderdale, FL 33314
greg@nova.edu

ABSTRACT

Research into predicting long-term resource needs has been faced with a very difficult problem of extending the accuracy period beyond the immediate future. Business forecasting has overcome this limitation by successfully incorporating the concept of human interaction as the basis of prediction patterns at the hourly, daily, weekly, monthly, and yearly time frames. Computer resource utilization is also impacted by human interaction therefore influencing research into predictability of resource usage based on human access patterns. Emulated human web server access data was captured in a feasibility study that used time series analysis to predict future resource usage. For prediction beyond several minutes, results indicate that the majority of projected resource usage was within an 80% confidence level thus supporting the foundation of future resource prediction work in this area.

Categories and Subject Descriptors

D.4.8 [**Performance**]: Measurements, Modeling and Prediction, Monitors;

General Terms

Design, Experimentation, Human Factors, Management, Measurement, Performance, Reliability, Security, Theory.

Keywords

Prediction methods, Demand forecasting.

1. INTRODUCTION

Researchers have been developing methods to provide more accurate computer resource predictability to support improvements in scheduling processes, managing disk IO, and quality of service [1, 5, 6, 8, 9]. This desire to find a more effective method to manage resources has led researchers to explore the predictability of resource usage patterns. Near-term utilization prediction solutions have often provided improvements over previous methodologies [1, 5, 7, 16, 18, 19]. However, the farther into the future a methodology attempts to predict

utilization, the less accurate it becomes. Thus research in computer system usage has focused on recent history to predict the near future utilization of the resource. However, business prediction models focus on longer time frames.

The domain of business trend prediction has used resource utilization forecasting to help determine just-in-time manufacturing, employee scheduling, inventory delivery, traffic flow analysis, high-temperature and low-temperature predictions, and mass transit scheduling. These business cases do not experience the lack of extensibility to longer-term predictions as seen in current methods used for predicting computing resource utilization. Because the research methods used by business for long term prediction focus on human interaction patterns they may provide opportunities for Information Technology (IT) researchers to adapt these techniques to help predict computing resource needs for processing, communications, and storage management.

The remaining sections of the paper will address the following: section two will address the current research being conducted in computing and business, section three will discuss the need for the proposed research, section four will provide observational evidence supporting the assertion, section five discusses the setup of a feasibility experiment, section six provides the results of the feasibility experiment, section seven provides theoretical benefits from the research, and section eight discuss future computer resource prediction research.

2. CURRENT RESEARCH

2.1 Computer Resource Management

Operating system scheduling has been a research topic of interest since early operating systems implemented multitasking [18]. Current scheduling algorithms use basic mathematical formulas to determine how to order the resource access. More complicated formulas are reserved for special needs, since the overhead of making the choice often outweighs the benefit gained from the selection [18]. It is very difficult to predict the utilization of a resource by an unknown process or the length of time that a process requires a resource. Research has shown that, as resource loads increase, scheduling algorithms become unfair [19]. Thus the provision of additional resource utilization information may improve upon an algorithms ability to provide an increase in fairness to running tasks. Research remains active in web scheduling [1, 7, 16]. The theme of this research domain is to increase the efficiency of web service responses to provide improved turnaround on tasks. Thus web service load balancing is improved by leveraging operating system scheduling with the addition of utilization prediction.

Andreolini and Casolari [1] focused their research on recognizing larger patterns in resource trends. By looking at the recent past they determined that processing needs could be determined using a reasonable prediction pattern such as increasing, decreasing, staircase, or alternating. By better understanding load trends Andreolini and Casolari [1] could provide advanced notice of overloading, offloading, or stabilization leading to better management of load balancing, admission control, scheduling, and graceful degradation.

Google has also recognized the need for its systems to react well in a highly fault-ridden environment [7]. The primary concern is hardware failure, but Google also recognizes that software can be "buggy" or have faults that create availability issues. Failure is deemed a normal state in systems and thus a variety of prevention techniques are used to keep the services active. Thus increased reliability is provided through fault tolerance aided by usage data obtained in the monitoring process.

Schroeder and Harchol-Balter's [16] web server work supports issues with heavily loaded systems noted by Ghemawat et al. at Google [7]. The work recognizes that at times web services may experience transient overloads attributed to events such as national television recognition or a newspaper article. While unpredictable events present random loads on the web servers, other events such as holidays also cause increased loads that are difficult to predict using current research. To help reduce the loads during excessive utilization, the Shortest-Remaining-Process-Time (SRPT) scheduling algorithm is used to estimate the remaining process time for web requests and, when appropriate, raises a process's priority to allow that process to complete more quickly [16]. Schroeder's research monitors system bandwidth usage to determine if SRPT is an improvement over existing web response scheduling methods used in an unmodified system. Both Schroeder's [16] and Google's [7] research have taken a reactive posture over a preventative posture.

2.2 Distributed Resource Management

Load balancing [14], resource requirements [5], and performance [10] research establishes a management framework that is enhanced by prediction. The methods use data collection and prediction techniques to identify resource-scheduling algorithms that improve scheduling effectiveness over current methods.

The Resource Prediction System (RPS) [5] is based on a collection mechanism that considers the cost of collecting the information for prediction could outweigh the benefits of that prediction. Thus, as the RPS toolkit records readings from the system, those numbers are fed into a predictive algorithm that is used to determine the resource's utilization up to approximately 30 seconds into the future.

Most predictive systems use the measurement of mean, median, and standard deviation of recent usage data from the target resources. Istin et al. [10] expanded on Dinda's [6] work, using wave analysis. Like previous work, Istin's focuses on common resources including memory, CPU statistics, disk IO, and communications. In this research, [10] short-term predictions were used over long-term predictions because the authors believe that prediction over the next few seconds for a distributed system is much more important that being able to predict several hours into the future.

Rood and Lewis [14] focused their work on failure prediction. To create the predictor, Rood and Lewis established a state machine that permits the predictor to move between five states:

- system available,
- CPU threshold exceeded,
- job eviction,
- user present,
- and system unavailable.

The probability of the appropriate state is calculated for the target machine using predictors based on the time a process is expected to take. Rood and Lewis [14] did not indicate the amount of history collected from the machine, but they used enough data to identify transitions between states. These transitions resulted in a Markov chain that identifies the probability of a state change. Rood's method was able to provide reasonable predictability of a machines state for about 16 days which improved machine resource use.

2.3 Business' View of Predictability

Business has used resource forecasting for a variety of needs, including traffic flow [9] and short-term water usage [13]. Both Haung [9] and Liu [13] identify a block of data to define a history of resource utilization and these data blocks are used to predict future resource utilization.

In Haung's [9] work, statistics generated from two months of traffic patterns for a toll road were used as a historical base. The traffic data was processed and provided a successful prediction of traffic flow over seven days because human interaction is frequently predictable.

In Liu et al's [13] work, a history of water utilization was collected for approximately six months in one-hour increments. This then provided a single day of predicted use, in which the prediction was compared to the actual use. Liu's research showed that human interaction creates an environment where forecasting can identify future water use over a single day.

In no case is the use of forecasting 100% accurate. Just as Haung's [9] and Liu's [13] research showed predictability over days or weeks is feasible, studies into computing resource use based on similar techniques may show that hourly, monthly, and yearly trends can be reasonably predicted due to human generated access to applications and systems.

3. THE NEED FOR RESEARCH

Computer science algorithms are targeted to control process and resource management, however low-level raw measurement of these resources is deemed random instead of predictable [1]. This is supported by the concept that computers execute many instructions per second, perform multiple context changes between tasks, and service many interrupt responses that predictability becomes difficult. Reinforcement of the randomness of task execution is supported by studies in process selection, resource management, and system communication which show predicting the future state of a computer is very difficult and probably is likely beyond determination.

Attempts have been made [5, 15] to review resource utilization and then apply those observations to predicting the future state of computer system resource utilization. Although there is some success, predictions have not been accurate beyond several minutes. As a result, disk IO, process, and other methods of scheduling are evaluated based on inconclusive results of efficiency thus simplicity guides the ultimate choice of algorithm [12].

The relative execution timeframe for a computer system and a user is very different, thus this difference in time perception should lead to a new direction in the focus of research. Scheduling is done at the system task level and as seen earlier in the discussion has been the time frame used for research on the topic of resource prediction. The review of research in this area has revealed the problem is extremely difficult due to the vast amount of information required to make a prediction. Servers can remain active for months; current research has not considered this large timeframe when reviewing resource utilization.

Research into computers and human behavior has crossed paths [2, 9, 13], but focuses on human patterns instead of the computing patterns. The timeframe of minutes, hours, days, weeks, months, years, and even decades is important to people and their associated tasks. This human timeframe also has no interest in how the computer completes a task, the resources used, or the processes involved in getting the work done. Thus this area can be further explored to adjust the focus of the research in resource predictability to time frames that are better suited to the nature of human and computer task interaction.

4. SUBJECTIVE EVIDENCE

Research supporting longer prediction timeframes has been used to train and predict patterns that contain human interaction [9, 13]. Patterns of usage exist in many other places such as in national phone usage on mother's day, gasoline usage over the summer, heating fuel usage during the winter, electric utilization for air conditioning during the summer, and passenger traffic at the airports between Thanksgiving and New Year's Day. While this research [9, 13] deals with traffic patterns or water usage, there are human patterns that also exist in computing that may also be predicted using similar methods. Businesses currently collect data to find patterns that can be more accurately provide pricing structures, inventory management, and staffing levels. Research hasn't been conducted into how long term computing patterns, generated by the user, drive resource utilization of that equipment.

One published example of patterns in computing use driven by people is a usage analysis of the 1998 World Cup Web Site [2]. Figure 1 clearly shows that shortly after the start of a game, web site usage jumped and then quickly declined. The only exception was on Sundays. This pattern follows through the entire World Cup series, mapped on page 23 of Arlitt and Jin's report [2], the pattern repeats for each game over a 20 day period of the World Cup.

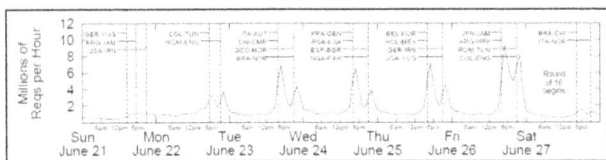

Figure 1: Workload Characteristics of 1998 World Cup Web Site

When a business opens, a pattern develops as the users log onto the system and begin their tasks for the first time each day. Additionally, disk utilization is likely to spike as well as Internet traffic as employees start the day and thus a pattern of use develops throughout the day.

Some colleges provide periodic class periods throughout the day, Monday through Friday of each semester. This class schedule creates very predictable network utilization based on student computer resource use. These patterns are generated by human interaction and are predictable [11], thus supporting the possibility that computer resource utilization is predictable in such cases based on the human timescale.

5. STARTING LONG-TERM PREDICTION

Research into long-term prediction must demonstrate that the basic premise of time-series analysis can be used for server resources before the more complex evaluations used by business can be applied to the process. To address the basics, a web server was set up using Windows 64-bit 2008 R2 Server operating system. This was loaded onto a Gateway E4300 (Intel Pentium 4 dual processor running at 3.4 Ghz). The server was also equipped with a Marvell Yukon Gigabit Ethernet interface and a Western Digital 1600JD ATA hard drive.

Both DNS and DHCP services were provided by the server for the client machines attached to a closed network for this experiment. These units were connected using a Cisco Catalyst 2950 48-port switch so they could access web content provided by IIS 7.0 web services. The raw data was collected on the server using a Windows LogMan, the command-line version of the GUI performance monitor program. LogMan was configured to capture CPU utilization, available memory, network traffic (in bytes per second) to and from the server, and the disk activity resulting from the requests sent to the web server. Each of these metrics was recorded in a log every ten seconds and a new log was started after each 24-hour period.

Twenty-two client machines were used for the initial research. These machines were Dell Precision T3500's with 64 bit openSUSE 11.2 installed on a Toshiba HDDR500E04X USB hard drive. The clients used an Intel Xeon 8-core CPU running at 2.8Ghz, a Broadcom NetXtreme gigabit Ethernet card, and eight gigabytes of RAM. The installation of openSUSE used the text-based interface to maximize the amount of RAM available to the simulator being used for the experiment.

The simulator selected for the experiment was Scalable URL Reference Generator (SURGE) created by Paul Barford [3] to exercise web servers. This simulator was selected after reviewing a number of current traffic generators because it not only exercises web services, but does so in a fashion that mimics human utilization of static web pages. While services have drastically changed since SURGE was created, the load put on the server is still able to provide a patterned level of requests to permit resources to be logged and evaluated for long-term predictability.

Barford [4] created a suite of programs with a variety of functions to emulate human trace data. The first program calculates the number of times a file will be accessed and the number of files the client may access on the server based on the most frequently-accessed document. A second program randomizes a file access list based on the Pareto distribution. Another program determines which files will be accessed as a single request and which files will be requested in a group using the pipelining feature available on web servers today. Another part of the suite will generate random wait times before the next request is made. In the original version this could be up to 15 minutes; however, modern servers set a two-minute timeout for connections that go quiet. The suite was adjusted so that no wait was longer than 90 seconds. Finally, the suite generates each of the files that will be used in the communication with random lengths of a single alphanumeric character. In Barford's [3] original version, every file contained "a"-s. For this experiment, it was desirable to exercise the server hard drive so that each client has its own character and set of files on the server.

The main purpose of SURGE is to generate requests and capture replies from the server. Barford's [3] focus was to create a workload generator that mimicked human behavior based on trace data, while this study will focus on using a controllable simulator to determine if long-term predictability is a viable research area. SURGE accomplishes its load generation by permitting up to eight processes to be started by the program, with up to 250 threads within each process. When each thread is running, it pulls a request from a common queue to generate a web GET statement. This is then transmitted to the web server using a standard TCP connection; the thread then reads the reply from the server. After the read is completed the thread pulls a sleep time from another common queue and waits for up to 90 seconds before initiating the next request. Initial runs indicated that a client could generate, and the server respond, to eight processes with 200 threads, making over 100,000 requests in about five minutes without difficulty.

Each of the SURGE clients was configured to run a request sequence every fifteen minutes using 75 threads. The first iteration starts eight processes and can complete 287,000 requests to the web server during its execution. The second iteration runs six processes, while the third iteration uses four processes and the fourth iteration uses two processes covering approximately 100,000 requests. Each iteration runs for a period of fourteen minutes with the remaining minute used to reset for the next iteration. A script was written to start SURGE in fifteen-minute iterations, restarting the four part sequence every hour. Each iteration level produces an average level of 35%, 28%, 21%, and 14% CPU utilization.

6. FEASABILITY OF FORECASTING

For this short study sample data was collected from the web server every ten seconds over a forty hour period by the LogMan program. The data samples were averaged into one-minute data points before being evaluated to determine if the data was a good fit for long-term forecasting. SAS was used to examine the data distribution for each minute, correlated hour-by-hour, over the forty-eight hours of data.

Each fifteen-minute load level shows a tight CPU utilization load generated by the simulator. These levels often remain within several percent of the mean. The server's clock was two to three minutes faster than the client's, providing the shift (see Figure 2) that accounts for the step-down pattern generated by the simulator. At the end of each fifteen-minute cycle the reset time is also evident within the minute pattern.

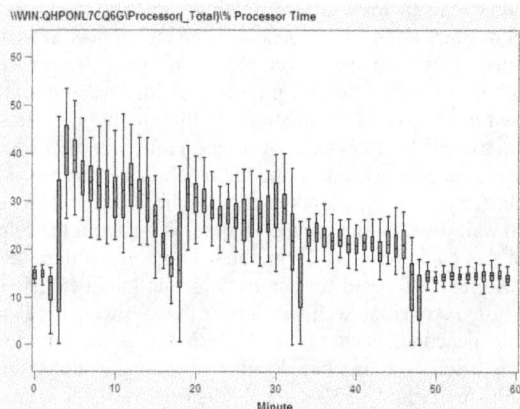

Figure 2: Box with Whiskers for CPU utilization

An additional evaluation was done using linear regression with an 80% confidence banding to provide evidence that the use of an appropriate seasonal evaluation will support the predictability of resources. In this case a single minute – minute 55 – was extracted from each hour over the forty-eight hour period and used to plot out the CPU utilization level of the server (see Figure 3). This minute had a mean of 14.44% and a standard deviation of 1.21%. As the figure indicates, only three samples of CPU utilization were outside the 3.1% range representing an 80% confidence level. The trend line and data distribution provide evidence that forecasting good fit based on the correlation of time and CPU utilization, and that time series analysis may provide an effective forecasting method.

The information provided in sections 5 and 6 is provided as foundation for the need for a much larger body of work. Time-series analysis has been widely used for business forecasting for years. Research toward an understanding of the patterns of computer resource utilization outside of operating system management has not received much attention. Additionally, work lags in predictions that attempt to look beyond several minutes into the future. The system described in section 5 was established to begin the feasibility of using time-series analysis for system resources over long-term periods.

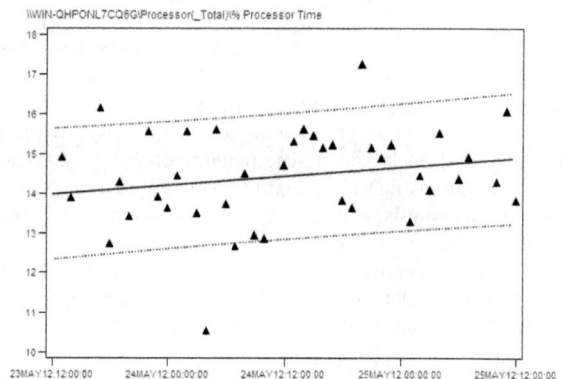

Figure 3: Scatter Plot for one minute over two days.

7. POSSIBLE RESEARCH BENEFITS

Since identifiable patterns already exist for resources, researchers can begin to identify how long-term resource predictions can be accomplished. Future research will focus on predictable use over hours, days, weeks, months, and years instead of only over the next few computing cycles. Once researchers begin to understand where human patterns influence resource utilization, additional IT research will open a variety of benefits to business and systems management.

Given a qualified forecasting system an administrator could identify periods-of-service overload for a web server, so that extra traffic could be diverted to another machine within the system. The administrator would use the history of the web server over the past several months while forecasting could identify times when an overload is likely to occur. The extra services could be deployed shortly before the overload is expected and released once the need has abated. A process of renting services from the cloud for a short time could reduce the cost of having a second system always on standby or by understanding when new systems would need to be added to accommodate growing needs.

At present, resource utilization is considered unpredictable and chances of predicting future utilization appears nearly random.

But with this type of research, some of the resource utilization should be predictable. For example, if the evaluation determines that CPU utilization during the organization's startup period each day, Monday through Friday, normally jumps to 60% and, of that 60%, 30% can be directly attributed to user logins with a ±2% deviation, a "random" CPU utilization of 30% would remain. That last 30% could then be bounded with acceptable deviations so that when the utilization moves outside those bounds, the system would be considered to be behaving abnormally. Then research could focus on another predictable event in the remaining 30% to reduce the randomness further. Eventually research would be able to identify the true randomness within the system and when that system was not acting predictably.

Initially the randomness of any resource utilization will be very large, but as more human generated patterns are discovered, that deviation will shrink and system resource use prediction will rise. By shrinking the remaining randomness of the system resources, a set of probabilities about the state of the machine can be determined (Figure 4). The wellness of a machine can be determined by three states: normal, abnormal, and failure. While resource utilization remains within the acceptable deviation of the prediction, the system remains in the normal state. If the resource utilization falls outside the prediction and deviation, the machine would move into an abnormal state. If the resource returns to utilization between the predicted use and deviation the machine can return to the normal state. Finally, if the machine experiences a hard or soft failure, it would move into the failure state.

Research begins with identifying the common patterns within a system. These could include network traffic patterns, Internet utilization patterns, and web service patterns. As more resources and utilization patterns are identified, the more administrators will be able to balance system health. Research then moves to creating a feedback loop that provides the system with the ability to make future predictions based on the original history plus the resource utilization as it has occurred in real time. In this way, hourly, daily, weekly, monthly, and yearly patterns can be updated to reflect patterns as they change based on human interaction.

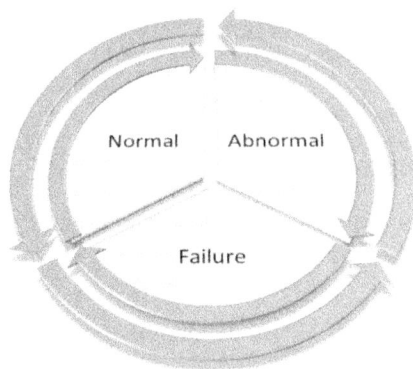

Figure 4: Machine States under Predictable Usage.

Once the forecasting research begins identifying resource utilization, a wide variety of additional research and management opportunities will arise.

- Load balancing could now add the additional dimension of expected resource load, permitting businesses to rent services for short periods after transferring critical data to the rented system.
- Distributed systems could use the forecasting to better balance process loads and, if a machine entered an

abnormal state, begin preemptive measures to move critical tasks prior to failure or overload.
- Services could be more properly sized to equipment and provide growth projections for a system retirement or upgrade.
- Virtual machines with opposite resource utilization could be safely matched together to save on hardware costs.
- Survivable systems could begin graceful degradation upon entering the abnormal state and restore full services if the machine returned to the normal state.
- Intrusion Detection/Prevention systems could begin more aggressive scanning upon entry to the abnormal state.
- Resource load prediction could identify the tipping points for the overloading of a resource and take preventative measures as the resource approaches that threshold.

8. CONCLUSION

Five to ten minute prediction methodologies based on computing time frames have been reasonably successful [1, 5, 11, 17], while similar results in longer patterns of resource utilization and prediction remain elusive. System degradation and overloading of services is a constant issue for the service owners that needs to be addressed to guarantee availability [8]. Web services continue to be a key area of interest due to the rate of growth and importance to industry [17]. Additionally, to support Quality of Service issues web services require better resource management. To address these concerns, Internet services should embrace resource prediction by shifting from short-term to long-term time periods. The results of these methods will provide improvements in load balancing, job dispatching, job distribution, and overload prevention [1] by permitting a system to better anticipate resource needs further into the future.

Algorithms currently use real time sampling [5] to solve resource limitation issues and can only address problems as they are detected or based on short-term prediction. The results of research in the area of short-term prediction of resource utilization, has been helpful in supporting scheduling changes [16], load balancing [17], and resource trending [1]. But, researchers have determined that current methods of data collection and analysis deteriorate quickly the further into the future predictions are made [1] and that more research into longer-term prediction is needed to manage system components.

Through the understanding of predictable human computer usage, the state of a machine can be determined. There will always be a small part of randomness in systems as patterns change over time. But business already understands the value of forecasting and knows that research based on human utilization patterns has tremendous value to improving business performance. Computing is no different: it is also driven by predictable human patterns.

Once those patterns are understood, administrators will be able to see which of the three states their equipment currently occupies. Knowing that equipment has entered an abnormal state will provide additional time to react to circumstances instead of reacting only after the system has entered a failing state.

Computer engineer's focus on computing electronics, the computer scientists focus on efficiencies of algorithms and systems, while IT has focused on effective use of equipment and services. The ability to effective use resources, balancing cost with need, keeping systems alive and protecting data during failures all fall into the concerns of IT. This type of research advances the effectiveness of equipment and services and therefore should be a research concern for those in IT.

9. REFERENCES

[1] Andreolini, M. and S. Casolari, *Load prediction models in web-based systems*, in *Proceedings of the 1st international conference on Performance evaluation methodolgies and tools*. 2006, ACM: Pisa, Italy. p. 27.

[2] Arlitt, M. and H. Jin, *Workload Characterization of the 1998 World Cup Web Site*, in *HPL-1999-35 (R.1)*. 1999, HP Laboratories Palo Alto. p. 90.

[3] Barford, P. and M. Crovella, *Generating representative Web workloads for network and server performance evaluation*. SIGMETRICS Perform. Eval. Rev., 1998. **26**(1): p. 151-160.

[4] Barford, P.R., *Modeling, Measurement and Performance of World Wide Web Transactions*, in *Graduate School of Arts and Sciences*. 2001, Boston University: Boston.

[5] Dinda, P.A., *Design, Implementation, and Performance of an Extensible Toolkit for Resource Prediction in Distributed Systems*. IEEE Transactions on Parallel and Distributed Systems, 2006. **17**: p. 160-173.

[6] Dinda, P.A. and D.R. O'Hallaron, *Host load prediction using linear models*. Cluster Computing, 2000. **3**(4): p. 265-280.

[7] Ghemawat, S., H. Gobioff, and S.-T. Leung, *The Google file system*, in *Proceedings of the nineteenth ACM symposium on Operating systems principles*. 2003, ACM: Bolton Landing, NY, USA. p. 29-43.

[8] Hoffmann, G.A., K.S. Trivedi, and M. Malek. *A Best Practice Guide to Resources Forecasting for the Apache Webserver*. in *12th Pacific Rim International Symposium on Dependable Computing (PRDC'O6)*. 2006.

[9] Huang, J. *Short-Term Traffic Flow Forecasting Based on Wavelet Network Model Combined with PSO*. in *International Conference on Intelligent Computation Technology and Automation*. 2008.

[10] Istin, M., A. Visan, F. Pop, and V. Cristea. *Decomposition Based Algorithm for State Prediction in Large Scale Distributed Systems*. in *Ninth International Symposium on Parallel and Distributed Computing*. 2010. Istanbul, Turkey

[11] Krithikaivasan, B., Y. Zeng, K. Deka, and D. Medhi, *ARCH-based traffic forecasting and dynamic bandwidth provisioning for periodically measured nonstationary traffic*. IEEE/ACM Trans. Netw., 2007. **15**(3): p. 683-696.

[12] Lampson, B.W., *Hints for computer system design*, in *Proceedings of the ninth ACM symposium on Operating systems principles*. 1983, ACM: Bretton Woods, New Hampshire, United States. p. 33-48.

[13] Liu, J., R. Zhang, and L. Wang. *Prediction of Urban Short-Term Water Consumption in Zhengzhou City*. in *International Conference on Intelligent Computation Technology and Automation*. 2010. Changsha, Hunan, China.

[14] Rood, B. and M.J. Lewis. *Resource Availability Prediction for Improved Grid Scheduling*. in *Fourth IEEE International Conference on eScience*. 2008.

[15] Rood, B. and M.J. Lewis. *Availability Prediction Based Replication Strategies for Grid Environments*. in *10th IEEE/ACM International Conference on Cluster, Cloud and Grid Computing*. 2010. Melbourne, VIC, Australia.

[16] Schroeder, B. and M. Harchol-Balter, *Web servers under overload: How scheduling can help*. ACM Trans. Internet Technol., 2006. **6**(1): p. 20-52.

[17] Sharifian, S., S.A. Motamedi, and M.K. Akbari, *An approximation-based load-balancing algorithm with admission control for cluster web servers with dynamic workloads*. J. Supercomput., 2010. **53**(3): p. 440-463.

[18] Silberschatz, A., P.B. Galvin, and G. Gagne, *Operating Systems Concepts, sixth ed.* 2003: John Wiley & Sons, Inc;.

[19] Wierman, A. and M. Harchol-Balter, *Classifying scheduling policies with respect to unfairness in an M/GI/1*, in *Proceedings of the 2003 ACM SIGMETRICS international conference on Measurement and modeling of computer systems*. 2003, ACM: San Diego, CA, USA. p. 238-249.

www.ingramcontent.com/pod-product-compliance
Lightning Source LLC
Chambersburg PA
CBHW051231200326
41519CB00025B/7337